D0905452

GREEK PORTRAITS IN THE J. PAUL GETTY MUSEUM

by Jiří Frel

14. Thespis (?)
75.AA.67.
From the Hauran. Hauran basalt,
H: 29.5 cm.

Photography by Donald Hull and Penelope Potter
Design by John Anselmo Design Associates, Santa Monica
Art Direction, Tom Lombardi
Production, Carol LaFayette
Type set by Freedmen's Organization, Los Angeles
Printing by Alan Lithograph Inc.

ISBN no. 0-89236-032-1
LC no. 81-83742

Library of Congress Cataloging in Publication Data
J. Paul Getty Museum.
Greek portraits in the J. Paul Getty Museum.
Catalogue: p.
Includes index.
1. Portrait sculpture, Greek—Catalogs. 2. Greece—Biography—Portraits—Catalogs. 3. Portrait sculpture, Roman—Catalogs. 4. Portrait sculpture—California—Malibu—Catalogs. 5. J. Paul Getty Museum—Catalogs. I. Frel, Jirí. II. Title.
NB1296.3.J18 1981 733'.3'074019493 81-83742
ISBN 0-89236-032-1 AACR2

TABLE OF CONTENTS

PREFACE

The collection of Greek portraits in the J. Paul Getty Museum—fifty-three pieces in this catalogue—is the largest in the western hemisphere. It includes the faces of numerous famous Greek men in Roman copies and also several Greek originals of the highest artistic quality. Some of these masterpieces are identified with famous individuals, like Alexander the Great, while others remain anonymous, such as the Getty Bronze. Several portraits are of considerable scholarly interest: for example, the museum's small bronze bust inscribed *MENANDROS* settled the long-disputed identity of this Greek poet, and a marble head known in two other replicas provided an opportunity to recognize the image of Xanthippos, father of Perikles, the great leader of Athenian democracy.

Greek portraits remind us of an unsung modern debt to ancient Greece. While the atom, electronics, astronomy, surgery, democracy, ethics, and poetry are still identified by their original Greek names, there are also many instances where the word is different but the substance follows an ancient Greek prototype. The concept of and respect for the individual, an essential ingredient of our way of life, was first developed by the ancient Greeks. Very often images of the immediate past are cast on Greek models; for example, Houdon's *Washington* follows this classical tradition. Keeping those ancient roots in mind, let us look at the museum's collection of Greek portraits.

The publication could have been realized only with the manifold help of the Getty Museum staff. The conservation of antiquities always provides the basis of future work, and with the Greek portraits, Zdravko Barov, Mark Kotansky, and Jerry Podany were especially involved. The photographs are by Donald Hull and Penelope Potter. Teri Howard typed and retyped the manuscript with unfailing patience. I owe them my sincere thanks. Marit Jentoft-Nilsen provided constant support. Without the unselfish and enthusiastic help of Sandra Knudsen Morgan, the work would never have been achieved; the text owes countless improvements and many ideas to her. My wife was, as always, my best critic.

J. F.
curator

THE STORY OF GREEK PORTRAITS

Representations of individuals appeared in antiquity long before Greek civilization, but one could hardly call the official images of Egyptian and Near Eastern rulers portraits in our sense of the word. They were created by religious and political considerations to support the social structure, with no real interest in the individual or his actual likeness. Their main aim was as a guarantee of the subject's survival for eternity, as we can interpret from the feelings expressed in many inscriptions which curse possible usurpers who might change the features or replace the original owner's name with another.

Portraiture may be characterized as the artistic depiction of an individual, starting with physical appearance but also emphasizing the individual's interior life, thoughts, and emotions, in the frame of the social context. This means that the image is determined by the views of its society. To create portraiture, a society has to have a positive approach to the individual; and its art has to reach a certain level of maturity. Consequently, some historical periods and communities, like the Celtic world in antiquity, the early medieval period, or the so-called primitive tribes did not need "real" representations of individual features. For the modern West, with the mechanical means of photography at our disposal, portraits automatically emphasize actual likeness. The first aim of portraiture for us seems to be identification, even though photographic achievements may transcend the external appearance of a single moment.

The ancient Greeks stressed much more the social idea, with portrait images of the perfect, heroic, godlike citizen than the uniqueness of a single individual. From the very commencement of Greek history, the aim of portraiture was to ennoble individual appearance, raising it to a perfection that was not only artistic and aesthetic but also—and primarily—ethical. It was rightly stated about Kresilas, who at the apogee of Athenian democracy produced an Olympian image of Perikles, that his art *nobiles viros nobiliores fecit*, "has made noble men appear still more noble." Awareness of individual deviations from the ideal norm existed during this time but found artistic expression only in images of characters on the margins of society, both of mythology and civic life. Effigies of real people showing them "warts and all" are found only occasionally, as an underground trend, despite the social taboo.

From Homer through the classical democratic city-states of the fifth century to Alexander, competition, *agon*, was the essence of the Greek commur ity. There was a perpetual striving for excellence in sport, war, politics, or art. At the same time, the individualism which is an inevitable part of such competition was condemned by the Greeks as *hybris*, at least until the meteoric appearance of Alexander broke through tradition, allowing the transcendence of human limits as he reached into the sphere of the divine. But even Alexander's portraits remained mostly ideal, emphasizing his divine descent rather than personal features. They still depict a very ideal type of the ruler, with only secondary emphasis on the likeness of Alexander himself.

fig. 1

Figure 1. *Fragment of an Attic grave relief of a boxer. Mid sixth century B.C. Athens, Kerameikos Museum.*

Greek art reached its maturity in the late sixth century, but the ambivalent Greek approach to the individual can be traced long before in the literature. Even a tentative survey of the Greek presentation of the individual must start with the Homeric poems. Divine Achilles, intrepid Ajax, Agamemnon, king of golden Mycenae, and the blameless Trojan Hector—all are impeccable heroes. They are described as courageous, strong, first in battle (which in Homer consisted mostly of individual duels between heroes while the masses looked on passively), but at the same time extremely touchy about their honor, which was the basis of their social status. The Homeric heroes are prone to easy anger and fits of jealousy; not infrequently they seem to behave like spoiled boys. The adjective "god-like" is frequently appended to their names, and indeed they are described as standard, ideal characters. Slightly more individual features are given to old loquacious Nestor, first in counsel and indefatigable in remembering the prowesses of his younger years, or to the many-faceted Odysseus. Yet the only real individual is Thersites, an anti-hero par excellence. Described as

> bandy legged and went lame of one foot, with shoulders
> stooped and drawn together of his chest and above this
> his skull went up to a point with the wool grown sparsely upon it,

he appears as a true villain, always ready to say something nasty about the leaders. For his big mouth he finally receives a sound thrashing, to the joy and satisfaction—and possibly education—of the onlookers: individualism does not pay.

In fifth century B.C. tragedy, heroes remain god-like in appearance, behavior, and language. Only slaves and servants, like the shepherd in Sophokles' *Oidipous*, are permitted to use colloquial idioms, conferring on them specific personalities. But while *epos* and tragedy represent individualism as *hybris*, lyric poetry was already presenting another attitude by the end of the seventh century B.C. One of the first poets, Archilochos from Paros, speaks openly of his disappointment over his failed wedding plans, producing an inelegant invective against his prospective father-in-law. In another poem he describes without hesitation how he dropped his shield running away from battle—a shameless admission of desertion and cowardice unthinkable for a well-born Greek. At the end of the sixth century, the poet Hipponax—a cynical beggar, old and decrepit—freely reveals his vulgar feelings and petty problems. Tradition records Hipponax as the unwilling "sitter" of perhaps the first sculpted portrait: Boupalous and Athenis, sons of the Chian sculptor Archermos, produced a likeness of Hipponax so flagrant that he became the laughing stock of all Greece. The outraged poet answered with such vitriolic verses that the sculptors hanged themselves in despair over their reputations—or so tradition relates. There is no trace of the statue representing Hipponax; was it really a portrait? We can perhaps imagine him in the light of a Attic funerary relief of a boxer from the middle of the sixth century (fig. 1). The career of this sportsman must have been tough: his nose was broken more than once, and his swollen ears never had time to heal properly. Hipponax may have looked even more like a caricature.

fig. 2

fig. 3

fig. 4

Figure 2. ***Dwarves playing with a ball. From a Proto-Attic krater of the first half of the seventh century B.C. Formerly in Berlin.***

Figure 3. ***Orestes killing Aigisthos in front of Klytaimnestra. From the same vase as figure 2.***

Figure 4. ***Gorgo, architectural decoration. Ca. 570 B.C. Athens, Acropolis Museum.***

THE GREEK VIEW OF INDIVIDUAL PHYSIOGNOMY

Caricature, like portraiture, deviates from the ideal, well-balanced image of a person. It may or may not represent an individual, and its humor does not presuppose the same degree of mature artistic expression as an accomplished portrait. In Greek art, caricatural representations of mythological creatures, specifically those with negative connotations, first appear in the early seventh century B.C. Sometimes one may hesitate over whether these early caricatures are intentional or the result of a lack of artistic maturity. A Proto-Attic krater dating from the early seventh century illustrates both points. A pair of joyful dwarves (fig. 2) indubitably seek to be amusing, but the scene of Orestes killing Aigisthos in the presence of the nervous Klytaimnestra (fig. 3) shows cranky figures with ridiculous gestures in an incoherent composition; the result is amusing to our eyes, a kind of naive art, but this was certainly not the artist's intention.

A head of Gorgo (fig. 4) intended for early sixth century architectural decoration on the Acropolis can be called to some extent a caricature. During the following half century, Attic and Corinthian vase painters drew, clearly with satisfaction, figures of pygmy dancers where the intention to amuse seems to be quite evident. This trend continued through the end of the century, for example, in a sketch of a cripple (fig. 5); and into the fifth century in representations like the hunchback Aesop in conversation with a fox on a red figure cup of ca. 470 B.C. (fig. 6). Still later in the 440s, a fragment represents a dancing dwarf named Hippokleides (fig. 7), who borrowed his name from an Athenian famous a hundred years before. Aesop was a barbarian—a nonGreek—and the same caricatural method used for the deformed and mythical was used to emphasize the ethnic features of nonGreeks. A cup by the Hegesiboulos Painter, ca. 500 B.C., shows an aged Levantine (fig. 8). A masterpiece by the Pan Painter two decades later represents, with sharply characterized ethnic features, Egyptian soldiers being scared to death by Herakles (fig. 9).

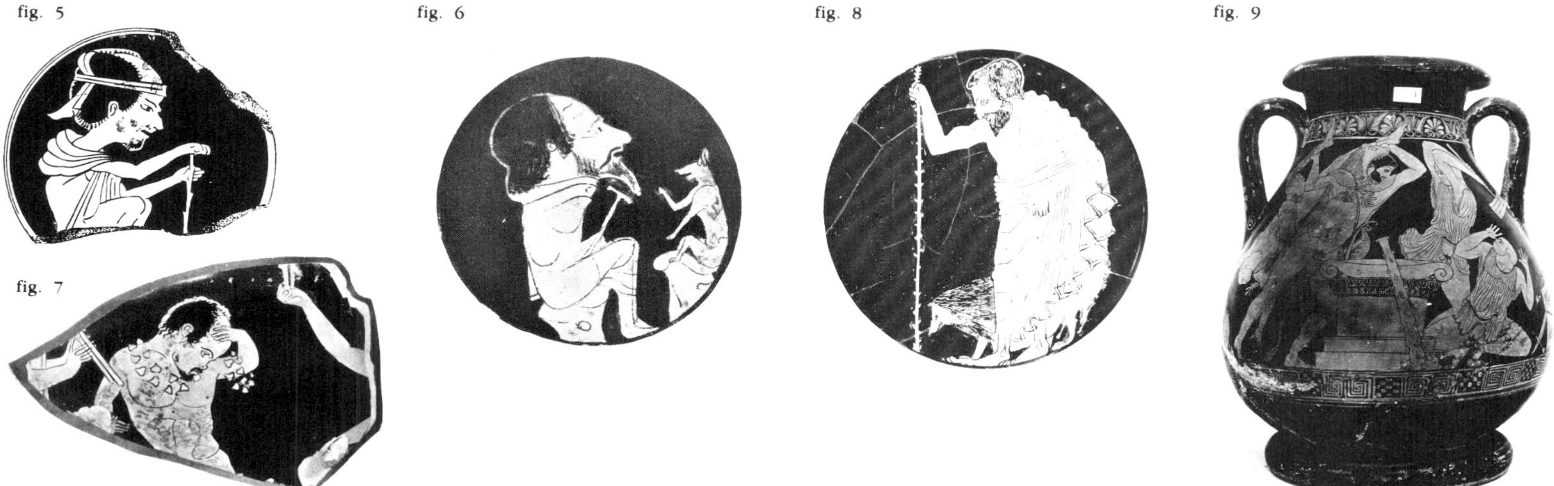

Slaves and servants also could appear "individualized." On a white-ground lekythos from about the middle of the fifth century, the dead mistress stands quietly near her grave monument in serene, ideal beauty, while a servant bringing offerings exhibits an astonishing profile with a big, upturned nose (fig. 10). Most slaves and servants were of barbarian origin. The Athenian policemen, for example, were state-owned slaves from Scythia; they must have been similar to a scary-looking warrior on a calyx Krater painted by the Achilles Painter ca. 460 B.C. (fig. 11). Old nurses were often Thracian; they are easily identified on Attic vases by the special scarification, wrongly called tattoos by archaeologists, on their upper arms and sometimes their cheeks. On a loutrophoros by the Painter of Bologna 228, ca. 470 B.C. (fig. 12) is an old nurse crying over her deceased beautiful, young mistress. Elsewhere the very old Geropso, dessicated and bent by age, carries with grandmotherly care the lyre of his charge, the spoiled infant Herakles, accompanying him to his music lesson (skyphos by the Pistoxenos Painter ca. 460 B.C., fig. 13). The name indicates that the potter must have been of barbarian origin himself: *pistos xenos*, "faithful foreigner," probably to be identified with Syriskos, "a small Syrian," as both names appear together on two vases. Other barbarians are attested as slaves in the pottery trade by their names, for example, *the* Lydian, Skythes, Brygos, and Epiktetos—"newly purchased."

Figure 5. *Cripple on an Attic red figure fragment. End of the sixth century B.C. Found on the Acropolis. Athens, National Museum.*

Figure 6. *Aesop talking with a fox. Interior of an Attic red figure cup. Ca. 470 B.C. Vatican.*

Figure 7. *Dancing dwarf named Hippokleides. Attic red figure fragment of ca. 440 B.C. Erlangen, University.*

Figure 8. *Levantine old man with his dog. Interior of a cup by the Hegesiboulos Painter. End of the sixth century B.C. New York, The Metropolitan Museum of Art.*

Figure 9. *Herakles killing Egyptian soldiers. Attic red figure pelike by the Pan Painter. Ca. 480 B.C. From the Acropolis. Athens, National Museum.*

fig. 10

fig. 11

fig. 12

fig. 13

Figure 10. *Servant at a grave. White-ground lekythos. 440–430 B.C. Berlin Museum.*

Figure 11. *Old warrior of barbarian origin. Attic red figure calyx krater by the Achilles Painter. Ca. 460 B.C. New York, The Metropolitan Museum of Art.*

Figure 12. *Old Thracian nurse. Attic red figure loutrophoros by the Painter of Bologna 228. Ca. 470 B.C. Athens, National Museum.*

Figure 13. *Old Geropso, nurse of Herakles. Attic red figure skyphos by the Pistoxenos Painter. Ca. 460 B.C. Schwerin, Museum.*

A cup signed by Phintias ca. 510 B.C., in the Getty Museum, is a virtuoso caricature of a naked woman, well along in years, represented with three spare tires around her middle, pendulous breasts, a triple chin, and an unflattering face (fig. 14). Even though an attractive appearance must generally have been essential to her profession, she could afford to be seen looking as she does: it surely would not harm her social reputation. Her impatient client must be Phintias himself and, of course, even in the intimate situation he retains the standard unmoved, ideal beauty customary for a Greek citizen. We may know the name—Syko—of this woman, as she appears with the name inscribed (fig. 15), this time well-dressed and playing the flute for the entertainment of numerous banqueters who include the vase painter Smikros, on a calyx krater by Euphronios of approximately the same date (fig. 18). She may have been popular among vase painters, but she presents us with a more important problem: does this caricature contain something of her actual likeness? The profile, with the triple chin and heavy cheeks, is indisputably the same, perhaps indicating a step towards portraiture.

Depictions of well-known individuals on vases can be traced from the end of the sixth through the first half of the fifth century. The best known example is Anakreon (born ca. 570), the lyric poet who came to Athens during the last decade of the Peisistratid tyranny. He quickly became a well-established public figure, the source of many folk legends after his death. He appears first as a lyre player on a cup from the penultimate decade of the sixth century. From the following decade onward, a scene in which he takes part occurs frequently on painted Attic pottery; it represents elderly men in women's dress, carrying parasols and even wearing earrings—a barbarian custom decried as effeminate by Anakreon himself. A lyre player among them is identified as Anakreon by an inscription in the earliest and best drawing (unfortunately fragmentary) by the

fig. 14

fig. 15

fig. 16

fig. 17

Kleophrades Painter. J. D. Beazley described the scene as that of Anakreon and his "boon companions." Another vase, also from the early fifth century, depicts the poet alone in a rather unsteady pose (fig. 16). Rather than showing an individual, the vase painter is repeating an anecdotal—and presumably topical—story, investing it with quasi-mythological character, comparable to a debauch of the drunken hero Herakles.

Several Attic vase painters in the early fifth century also depicted the poetess Sappho, a historical figure active only a century earlier. The most famous representation of her is on a cylindrical vase by the Brygos Painter, about 480 B.C. (fig. 17). It shows the poet Alkaios approaching his compatriot Sappho with a hesitant proposal; Sappho turns away with a gesture of refusal. The tale handed down about this meeting recounts that he was saying, "I want to tell you something, but I feel ashamed." She rebuked him, answering, "If it were anything correct, you wouldn't feel so." As with Anakreon and his cronies, the situation is captured in a lively fashion, but there is little if anything that can be perceived as portraiture in the faces of either poet.

Figure 14. *Old hetaira. Attic red figure cup signed by Phintias. Ca. 510 B.C. Malibu, The J. Paul Getty Museum.*

Figure 15. *Syko. Perhaps the same woman as in figure 14, but this time playing the flute at a banquet. Attic red figure calyx krater by Euphronios. Munich, Museum für antike Kleinkunst.*

Figure 16. *Anakreon. Attic red figure amphora by the Flying Angel Painter. Ca. 480 B.C. Paris, Louvre.*

Figure 17. *Sappho and Alkaios. Attic red figure kalathos by the Brygos Painter. Ca. 480 B.C. Munich, Museum für antike Kleinkunst.*

fig. 18

fig. 19

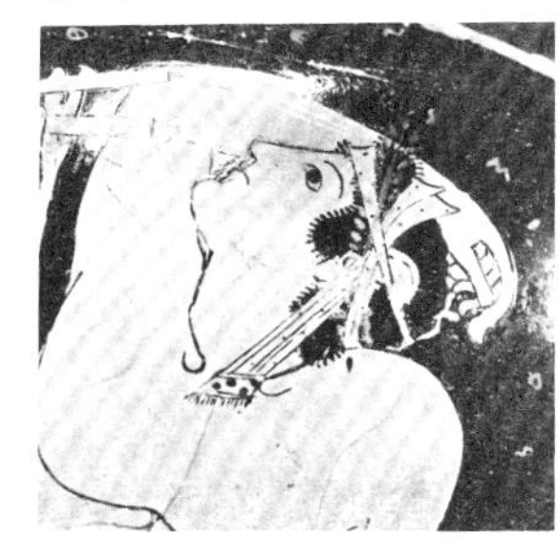

fig. 20

fig. 21

Figure 18. *Smikros. On the same calyx krater by Euphronios as figure 15 above.*

Figure 19. *Smikros. Attic red figure dinos by Smikros. Ca. 510 B.C. Brussels, Musée de Cinquantenaire.*

Figure 20. *Euphronios courting Leagros. Attic red figure psykter by Smikros. Before 510 B.C. Malibu, The J. Paul Getty Museum.*

Figure 21. *Dike (Justice) killing Adikia (Injustice). Red figure panel from an Attic bilingual amphora. Ca. 525 B.C. Vienna, Kunsthistorisches Museum.*

When the vase painters occasionally represent themselves, they appear in the frame of the same ideal types. We can compare the profile of Smikros done by his master Euphronios (fig. 18) with Smikros's own "self portrait" (fig. 19). They are practically contemporary, about 510. In neither case is there anything individual in the features: both just show a youth of good upbringing. The appearance is not important; the circumstances are. In both pictures, Smikros participates at a symposium, a joyful gathering of the Athenian *jeunesse dorée*. Slightly earlier, Smikros depicted Euphronios coveting the aristocratic boy Leagros—the famous beauty of his time (fig. 20). The drawing of the purely conventional figures is much less successful; Smikros was not a great artist, but his flattering intention was rather to publicize Euphronios's presence among the cream of Athenian society than to emphasize his beauty.

Another kind of representation, providing opposition of ideal and "real" figures, can be studied on an early bilingual neck amphora ca. 525 B.C. The red figure panel represents a fight between Dike and Adikia—Justice and Injustice (fig. 21). Dike is, of course, crushing her adversary. She is as perfectly turned out as if she had just left her toilette. She triumphs without effort, with a light grace, and her face reveals ideal beauty without any characterization. Injustice is shown uncombed, her dress disorderly and ungirdled. With her mouth wide open, she disgracefully screams her defeat. A direct parallel is the famous krater by Euphronios with Herakles strangling the giant son of Earth, Antaios (fig. 22). Again, neatly curled hair frames the hero's beautiful face as he wins with an ease suited to immortal gods. The collapsing Antaios does not know how to behave, letting a death rattle escape from the "fence of his teeth." His wild hair suits well his enormous nose and generally rather bestial expression.

fig. 22

fig. 23

fig. 24

Throughout the sixth century and even slightly before, individual names occur on sculpted votive offerings and on grave monuments. But even if an individual is depicted, there is not the smallest trace of any personal features. However, some differences in approach to individualism can be perceived. On the Greek mainland, sculptures are inscribed as an image or statue of so-and-so put on the grave by a mourning father or as an image of so-and-so dedicated, say, to Apollo. In East Greece, however, we find examples of statues speaking in the first person: "I am Chares, ruler of Teichousa. The statue belongs to Apollo." This is surely an expression of self-consciousness in the frame of a more tolerant community, perhaps also inspired by the pride of petty rulers in the orbit of Persia. A Latin literary source relating Hellenistic traditions about the votive statues of victors in the Olympic Games notes that in the case of a third victory statues erected afterward were called *iconic*. Modern scholarship has interpreted this word as implying individual likeness. As a matter of fact, it simply meant that the event in which an athlete achieved his victory could be shown. For example, a three-times victorious discus thrower could be depicted in an appropriate pose holding the discus, although the features of his face remained beautiful and impersonal.

On the whole, only undesirable mythological creatures or inferior elements of low status like barbarians or slaves could be given an individualized likeness. Gods, heroes, and their true kin—free Greek citizens—were limited to impersonal beauty. Revealing passion or any feelings was equally inadmissible. A young Athenian aristocrat, mortally wounded in battle, is represented on his grave relief of circa 520 with divine grace, his archaic smile provided with an almost Leonardesque intonation (fig. 23). His passing has become an apotheosis, and he achieves immortality as a divine hero. On the other hand, a centaur on a cup in Munich (Foundry Painter, ca. 480, fig. 24) expires in excruciating agony; he is allowed to be human.

Figure 22. *Herakles strangling Antaios. Attic red figure calyx krater signed by Euphronios. Ca. 510 B.C. Paris, Louvre.*

Figure 23. *The death of a young hero. Attic grave relief. Ca. 520 B.C. Malibu, The J. Paul Getty Museum.*

Figure 24. *Dying Centaur. Interior of a cup by the Foundry Painter, Ca. 480 B.C. Munich, Museum für antike Kleinkunst.*

fig. 25

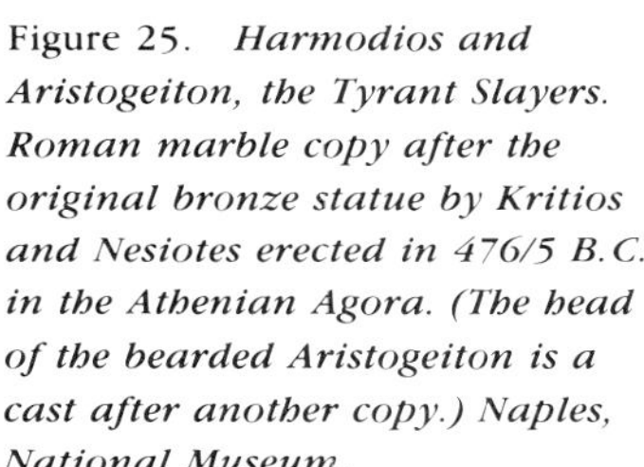

fig. 26

fig. 27

Figure 25. *Harmodios and Aristogeiton, the Tyrant Slayers. Roman marble copy after the original bronze statue by Kritios and Nesiotes erected in 476/5 B.C. in the Athenian Agora. (The head of the bearded Aristogeiton is a cast after another copy.) Naples, National Museum.*

Figure 26. *The group of the Tyrant Slayers, reproduced about 300 B.C. on the so-called Elgin Throne. Malibu, The J. Paul Getty Museum.*

Figure 27. *Head of Harmodios. Roman marble copy. Naples, see figure 25 above.*

THE FIFTH CENTURY

In the year 514 two Athenian aristocrats, Harmodios and Aristogeiton, friends and more than friends, were personally offended by Hipparchos, the younger son of the tyrant Peisistratos. They organized a conspiracy to overthrow the tyranny. On the agreed upon day of the Great Panathenaic festival, thinking they were betrayed, Harmodios, the younger of the conspirators, murdered Hipparchos and was immediately killed by Hipparchos's bodyguards; Aristogeiton perished later under torture. The investigation of the conspiracy included the interrogation of Leaina ("the lioness"), a hetaira, girlfried, of Aristogeiton. Under torture she bit off her tongue so as not to betray the secrets of her friends. In 510, the democracy succeeded the tyranny and the two aristocrats were elevated to the level of national heroes, perhaps with a public and intentional misunderstanding of their motivation. Songs were composed about them, and schoolchildren were bored for generations by the deed of these Tyrant Slayers. A statuary group of the two (fig. 25) was cast by a sculptor, Antenor, and placed prominently in the Agora, the central marketplace of Athens. According to some archaeologists this unveiling took place in the last decade of the sixth century, while others have dated it in the years immediately following the victory at Marathon in 490 B.C. No definite evidence exists, but we are told that in 480 Xerxes carried the group as booty from burning Athens to Persia. It was returned to Athens only by Alexander the Great or one of his successors. In 477/6 the Athenians had the group recast, possibly without noticeably modifying the original composition, by Kritios and Nesiotes, followers of Antenor in the same workshop. This was the first, and for close to a century, the only public monument to individuals erected by the city itself. The second version survives in several Roman copies. For more than a century archaeologists have gleefully quarreled about the original appearance of the group, reaching very creative if not always convincing reconstructions. For the original alignment of the two figures, the best witness is the small relief on the side of the Elgin Throne, now in the Getty Museum (fig. 26). The composition presents an ideal reconstruction of their action: the intrepid Harmodios attacks, while the equally courageous but bearded Aristogeiton covers his friend's flank. Both of the Tyrant Slayers are represented as perfectly beautiful (heads, figs. 27/28); the only distinction between the two is that Aristogeiton wears a full beard. On the whole, besides the fact of representing concrete individuals in definite action, the group continues the rather conservative Greek approach toward portraiture. This group was an exception to the rule against individual glorification that the Athenians allowed to be raised only for very specific reasons.

fig. 28

fig. 29

fig. 30

When the painted decoration of the Stoa Poikile was commissioned to represent the battle of Marathon, Miltiades' son Kimon proposed that his father and other commanding officers be identified by inscriptions. The Athenians voted against the idea. Kimon then suggested that the commanders be permitted at least some actual likeness. Even this compromising proposal was voted down. The public aversion to actual likeness was repeated when the commanders from another battle were allowed only to erect three commemorative herms with no personal features. On the other hand, Kimon was able to command the sculptor Pheidias to include a portrait of his father Miltiades in a statuary group commemorating Marathon in Delphi, far from the public opinion of the city. A pair of bronze statues, original Greek works, recently discovered in the sea close to the shore of South Italy, may have belonged to this or to a similar Pheidian group; they show some attempt at personal characterization and date before the middle of the fifth century (fig. 37).

Some other representations that must depict individuals belong to the same period. They express the contradiction between the collectivist feelings of Greek communities and the inevitable urge toward individualism and self-aggrandizement in the hearts of the citizens themselves. The first certain portrait, datable to the 70s of the century, is a head of an Athenian strategos, a general, wearing the characteristic Corinthian helmet (fig. 20). The bearded Aristogeiton is a good comparison even if this asymmetrical face, with the mouth at an oblique angle, is considerably more individual. Several copies have survived, but they are in poor condition. The best replica in Munich has been tampered with in modern times; a large part of the face is remodeled. A hitherto unpublished small-size replica in basalt (fig. 30) from Asia Minor, though undamaged, is small and of mediocre quality. Yet it serves to support the hypothesis that the so-called "oldest" strategos may be Themistokles, the ostracized Athenian statesman whose career ended in Asia Minor as a petty ruler thanks to the grace of the Persian king. The best replica shows a large face with a slightly drooping mouth.

Figure 28. ***Head of Aristogeiton. Roman marble copy (compare figure 25). Rome, Capitoline Museum.***

Figure 29. ***Athenian general: Themistokles (?). Roman marble copy after a bronze of 480/470 B.C. Munich, Glyptothek.***

Figure 30. ***Athenian general. Small Roman basalt replica of the portrait in figure 29. Smyrna, Museum.***

fig. 31 fig. 32

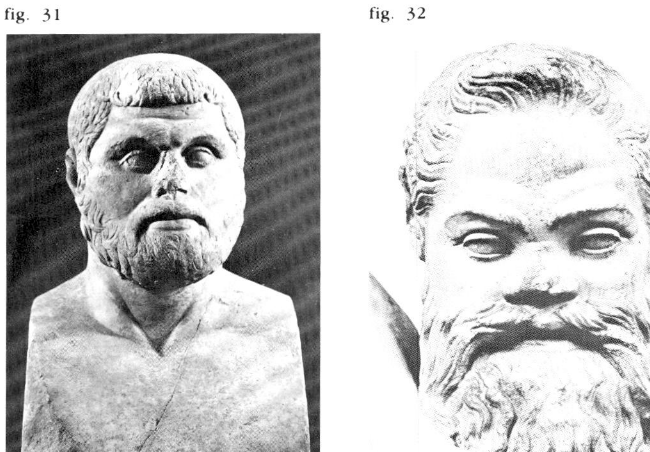

Figure 31. ***Themistokles. Inscribed Roman marble herm after a bronze original of 470/460 B.C. Ostia, Museum.***

Figure 32. ***Satyr Marsyas. Roman marble replica from the bronze statuary group by Myron after 450 B.C. Vatican.***

The same man may appear on the inscribed herm found in Ostia (fig. 31) some forty years ago, of which there is no replica. This herm provoked a spirited discussion about its date. It has been considered everything from a contemporary life portrait dating between 470/ 60 to an imaginary reconstruction of the third quarter of the fourth century B.C. when an image of Themistokles is recorded in the theatre of Dionysos in Athens together with other glories of the past to a Neoclassical creation of the first century B.C.; as a desperate proposal, the third century A.D. has even been suggested, which is indeed the date of the copy. There also is disagreement about where the original portrait of Themistokles stood. In Athens? Possibly in the sanctuary of Artemis the good advisor, built by Themistokles himself and thus his own dedication? In Argos,? where he began his exile, shaping a new constitution for that city? Or in his fief in Asia Minor, where his statue in heroic nudity appears on local coins in Roman times? What seems sure are the facts that the original was a private dedication because he does not wear a helmet, that the face is individual, showing an unflattering visage of penetrating intelligence, and that the herm is an extract from a portrait statue. We gain the impression that the man must have been short, and we can also see that the style belongs before the middle of the fifth century, whatever idiosyncracies or peculiar details may have been added by the copyist. The short cap of hair is treated similarly to Myron's Diskobolos, and the style of this sculptor is the closest possible parallel. In the established *oeuvre* of Myron there is a good attempt at characterization in the face (fig. 30) and figure of the Silen Marsyas, who is ecstatic as he catches the flute which Athena has just thrown away; for the first time, the animalesque face of a satyr is given a divine spark despite his natural ugliness.

fig. 33

fig. 34

fig. 35

A good acquaintance of Themistokles, the Spartan king Pausanias, provides another early portrait (fig. 33). Pausanias commanded the Greeks at Plataiai in 479, but ended his life condemned as a traitor. Walled up in the temple where he sought asylum, we are told that his own mother laid the first brick that starved him to death. Two statues of him were erected afterwards, as prescribed by the Delphic oracle in penance for allowing the desecration of the temple by his death. Several copies of the head survive, some of them indicating that there was a short mantle over the shoulder. The identity is confirmed by the special knot tied in the middle of his beard in the Persian style—a fashion that Pausanias avidly imitated. The face is simple but brutal and perhaps a little too "old" for the man; perhaps the excesses of his life prematurely aged him. The style seems to be Peloponnesian. One would like to compare the art to that of the centaurs of the west pediment of the temple of Zeus in Olympia. Several of these present excellent character studies of violent emotions: one old "devil" (fig. 34) with distorted grimacing looks like an attempt at some portrait-like individualization.

Still before the middle of the fifth century a Mikythos dedicated a statuary group in Olympia, the work of Dionysios of Argos, which included the first known image of Homer. This is recognized in the bearded head with closed eyes known to us from several Roman replicas. The best copy in Munich (fig. 35) shows mild, unindividualized features. The venerable age radiates a divine penetration of the universe. The closed eyes suggest the blindness. The best parallel for this head are the verses by which Homer himself introduced Demodekos, a fellow blind poet,

excellent singer,
whom the Muse had loved greatly and gave him both good and evil;
She reft him of his eyes, but she gave him the sweet singing
art.

Later centuries would petrify other visions of the Poet (see pages 27–28), but this Homer is perhaps not only the most classical but also the most Greek, and closest to the spirit of his poetry.

Figure 33. ***Pausanias. Roman marble replica after a bronze original of ca. 460 B.C. Rome, Capitoline Museum.***

Figure 34. ***Head of a Centaur from the west pediment of the temple of Zeus, Olympia. Before 460 B.C. Olympia, Museum.***

Figure 35. ***Homer. Roman marble copy after a bronze original by Dionysios of Argos before 450 B.C. Munich, Glyptothek.***

fig. 36

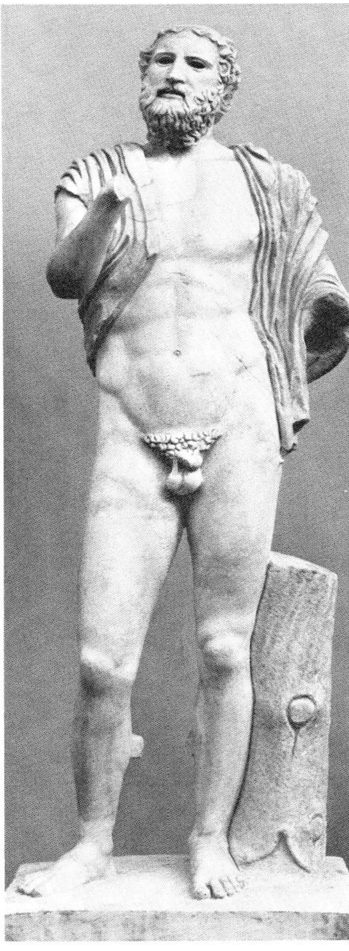

fig. 37

The next step in the development of portraiture comes in the mature classical age. We know from Pausanias' description of the Acropolis that a bronze statue of Anakreon stood alongside one representing Xanthippos. From the fact that the latter was Perikles' father, it was deduced that the group must have been dedicated by Perikles himself as a public memorial to the friendship between a successful commander and the popular poet-singer. The image of Anakreon is well known as one of the replicas is inscribed, and the best copy is a complete statue which shows the poet with a small mantle over one shoulder, holding his instrument, in heroic stance, the eyes turned heavenwards, performing in the divine inspiration of a glorious song (fig. 36). Still alive in the memory of the Athenians as drawn on vases as a humorous figure, a jolly fellow who exalted wine and love (fig. 16 above), in the Acropolis statue he was elevated to an ideal, ageless beauty analogous perhaps to Dionysos himself. One detail about the statue transcends the idealized appearance: Anakreon is infibulated in accordance with the belief that chastity improved not only the voices of singers but also the performance of athletes. The sculptor must have been Pheidias. The art corresponds to a figure on the shield of Athena Parthenos and to a slightly over life-size bronze (fig. 37) (one of a pair) fished from the waters off the tip of Reggio di Calabria in recent years, which in the articulation of the hair and beard and the delineation of physiognomy and anatomy is so like Anakreon that this bronze may be an original by Pheidias himself. The Xanthippos grouped with the Anakreon (fig. 38) on the Acropolis is identified by comparison with Anakreon: the only strategos of the same style (see no. 1, 2 and pp. 38–41 for the identification). Xanthippos is a hirsute man of soft but serious appearance. His identification throws new light on the question of individual physiognomy as the Greeks perceived it. In the twentieth century, we perceive hardly anything individual in his appearance, but for the classical Greeks it may have been very different.

fig. 38 fig. 39

The starting point for some general observations on the Greeks and actual likeness is the well-known image of Perikles (fig. 39), preserved in five replicas, two of them inscribed. The original must have been dedicated on the Acropolis by Perikles' son immediately after his father's death in 429 B.C. It was cast by Kresilas. Fragments of the original base with parts of the dedicant's name and the incomplete signature of the artist survive. There is a general agreement that this is perhaps the most classical and least personalized image of an individual created in the fifth century. Perikles died when he was slightly over seventy, but there is no trace of old age in the serene appearance of his face. The image really does justice to the adjectives "Olympian" and "Zeus-like" frequently given to the democratic leader during his lifetime. Some archaeologists would like to see a personal feature in the handful of hair showing through the top of the visor of the helmet: the contemporary comic poet Kratinos mocked Perikles with the epithet "onion-headed" for the immense vault of his skull.

Compared with Xanthippos' portrait, the art is completely different. The classicism of Kresilas' Perikles is precise, a self-sustaining style without any affectation, perhaps even a little dry. The earlier image of Xanthippos, on the other hand, is more richly modeled, with more emphatic expression and even some theatrical magnanimity. It is no wonder that some archaeologists dated the original of the Xanthippos to the end of the fifth century. On the other hand, everybody agrees that the visages of the two men are very close. We can go further: it is almost as if the two famous faces share a family likeness: Xanthippos and Perikles were father and son. The self-evident conclusion is that what appears to us as a strictly impersonal perfection of the classical type includes after all some individual characteristics which must have been perceptible to the Athenian viewers of the fifth century, even if they escape modern eyes.

Figure 36. *Anakreon singing. Roman marble copy after a bronze statue by Pheidias of before 450 B.C. Copenhagen, Ny Carlsberg Glyptotek.*

Figure 37. *Warrior. Original bronze statue probably by Pheidias. 460/450 B.C. Reggio di Calabria, National Museum.*

Figure 38. *Xanthippos. Roman marble head after a bronze statue by Pheidias of before 450 B.C. East Berlin, Pergamon Museum.*

Figure 39. *Perikles. Roman inscribed marble herm from Hadrian's Villa. After the bronze statue by Kresilas of after 429 B.C. London, British Museum.*

fig. 40

fig. 41

fig. 42

Figure 40. *Pheidias as Daidalos. Roman marble copy (the so-called Strangford shield) after the golden shield of Athena Parthenos by Pheidias of 438 B.C. London, British Museum.*

Figure 41. *Heads of an eagle, Zeus, and Pheidias on a carnelian. Second century A.D. Brno, Moravian Museum.*

Figure 42. *Profiles of Pheidias and his Zeus on a Roman gem. Early second century A.D. Private collection.*

Anakreon and Xanthippos were cast by Pheidias, and Pheidias played a much more important role in the development of the portrait than might be guessed from the historical sources and from the representations of individuals attributed to him. A tradition recounts that Pheidias inserted the likenesses of his friend Perikles and himself as participants in the battle against the Amazons represented on the golden shield of Athena Parthenos. Many archaeologists dismiss this tradition as a later (even if ancient) invention, but it seems that this sacrilegious action was used as a count of accusation against Pheidias by the political enemies of Perikles. It is related that Perikles was not too recognizable, as his face was covered by his arms raising a spear. Next to him on the best replica (fig. 40) is a bald man with a vigorous profile wearing a short tunic, the dress of an artisan, who is brandishing an axe. The face of the artisan is strongly characterized, one could even say individual: the marked cheekbones, heavy chin, massive nose, enormous dome of the skull, and even the stature are personal; he appears as a rather short and stocky, forceful character.

Of course, the story of the two images was a good one to develop in a historical anecdote. In the first century B.C. Cicero even noted credulously that Athena's shield was constructed in such a way that if someone removed the two "portraits," the whole cult statue would have collapsed. Evidently there was a feeling that the inclusion of the portraits was somehow "improper." Perhaps already before Cicero, a new story had appeared; Pheidias was seen not only as an accomplished artist but also as a shrewd wizard—a thaumaturgos or miracle worker. The legend lived long: on a magic gem from the second century A.D. found in South Moravia in Slavonic contexts of the ninth century A.D. (fig. 41), the subject is three heads united into one: eagle, Zeus, and a bald-pated, strong jawed man. Below it are two letters: PH (Pheidias) in Latin. A similar profile appears on another gem, together with Zeus, in a private collection (fig. 42).

Already in the fourth century B.C. the "self portrait" of Pheidias may have been rejuvenated by another sculptor. The unique replica of the head (fig. 43) shows a likeness very similar to the small relief on the shield

fig. 43 fig. 44  fig. 44  fig. 45

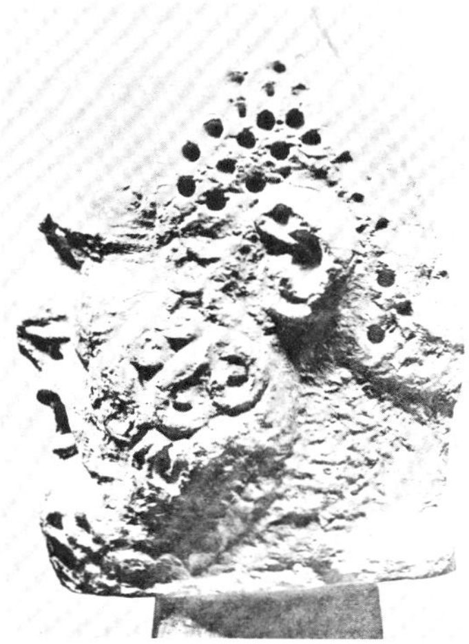

and to both gems. A large bronze statuette acquired by the Metropolitan Museum (fig. 44a–b) ten years ago emphasizes the same likeness in more detail. The short and stocky man is clearly represented as a craftsman; his short gown leaves the left shoulder free so that he can hold his hammer in that hand. His sketchbook is tucked in his belt, and he stands with crossed arms as if contemplating a finished work. The statuette may have been cast in the late second century B.C. The genre-like mood corresponds to Alexandrian art. In any case, we know that the Romans possessed an image of Pheidias: the base of a herm was found in Hadriain's Villa with feet and with Pheidias' name inscribed.

This is still not all. A type of head comparable to the profile on the Parthenos shield can be traced on the Parthenon itself, for example the severe figure of an elderly commander of cavalry in the Parthenon West frieze. A fanciful variant appears as a centaur (fig. 43, South metope IX) where the face is contracted in a painful grimace as his human opponent desperately tries to poke the centaur's eye out. Was Pheidias himself aware that some of his collaborators may have been making fun of his appearance? Or did he himself design it? However it may be, the hairy faces of the Parthenon centaurs, with a scale of animation ranging from brutal animality to noble resignation, could afford to appear more human that the divinized human figures. They constitute a true school of portraiture.

Figure 43. *Pheidias. Roman marble head after a fourth century B.C. bronze original. Copenhagen, Ny Carlsberg Glyptotek.*

Figure 44a and b. *Pheidias (?) Alexandrian bronze statuette with silver-inlaid eyes. Late second century B.C. New York, The Metropolitan Museum of Art.*

Figure 45. *Centaur head from the Parthenon, South metope IX. Before 440 B.C. London. British Museum.*

fig. 46

fig. 47

Figure 46. *Socrates. Roman marble copy after a bronze statue, perhaps by Apollodoros the Mad, from the early fourth century B.C. Naples, National Museum.*

Figure 47. *Socrates. Roman marble copy after a bronze statue by Lysippos set up in the Pompeion in Athens in the late fourth century B.C. Rome, National Museum.*

In condemning Pheidias for a sacrilegious *hybris*, the Athenians must have understood that the individualism expressed in personal features undermined the polis community. Indeed, the next steps in the attack on traditional values appear in the tragedies of Euripides and in the activity of the silenic wizard Socrates who brought philosophy from heaven to earth, questioning everything. A banquet including Socrates is described by Xenophon. The revellers, warmed by wine, began a beauty contest. The unquestioned winner is a beautiful boy until Socrates rises to participate in the contest, maintaining that his protruding eyes are more beautiful, as their visual angle is larger, and that his upturned nose is more lovely too, as it is able to enjoy smells from every direction. Someone adds ironically that Socrates' Silen-like swollen lips are indeed prettier—as the kiss may be sweeter and could even be given to two people at once! Something more serious of course lies behind this mockery. Not only is this a reappraisal of established aesthetics but it also suggests a new approach to the individual in general. Socrates' homely appearance was well-tailored for the case. In a more poetic way in Plato's *Symposium* Alkibiades, slighty drunk, praises his beloved master, stating that he is like the rustic sculptures of Silens that contain silver or gold divine images inside. The same dichotomy characterizes the two versions of Socrates' portrait. The first, executed probably immediately after his execution, correctly renders his unattractive exterior as that of an old satyr (fig. 46). There is little if any otherworldly sparkle. It is the uninspiring Socrates as seen by the pedestrian Xenophon, the ugly husband of Xanthippe. How different is the head of the statue cast more than a half century later by Lysippos (fig. 47)! It was commissioned by the repentant Athenians for the entrance of the Pompeion, the gathering place for holy processions to Eleusis. The face is clearly the same in this version, only the artist here reveals the divine Socrates of Plato's early dialogues, the great seducer of souls, the man whom the god of Delphi proclaimed to be the wisest of men.

fig. 48

fig. 49

fig. 50

THE FOURTH CENTURY

These individualistic trends were just beginning to appear both in sculpture and in other minor arts. The sculptor Demetrios of Alopeke is reputed in ancient tradition as a maker of men, often opposed to Pheidias, the maker of gods. But Pheidias may have been his teacher, as the art of characteristics inaugurated by Parthenon centaurs seems to have been developed in images connected with Demetrios. He is reputed to have created the statue of Lysimache, a nonagenarian priestess of Athena (fig. 48). Her expressive, ravaged head has been identified in two Roman copies. The original inscribed base survives in fragmentary condition. Recently a body bent by age was successfully connected with them, producing the first female portrait. Of the other portraits by Demetrios mentioned in literary sources, we have some visual idea about the statue of Pelichos, a Corinthian general. It was said to sport an ugly face, scant hair, and a protruding belly. There is a herm in cuirass which may be a Roman extract from this portrait (fig. 49), associated with several other heads. Demetrios' portraiture was sharp but limited to exterior appearance rather than seeking insights into the individual psychology of the sitter. The first version of Socrates' portrait is closely connected to this approach. One would like to attribute it to a sculptor who was Socrates' pupil in philosophy called Apollodoros ho Manicos (Apollodoros the Mad) as he destroyed most of his work because he was dissatisfied with it. Perhaps it should also be remembered that Socrates began as a sculptor himself and that his father was a woodcarver.

The beginning of Demetrios's career belongs already to the fifth century B.C. Several gems also datable to the late fifth century have portraits depicted on them. One of them, signed by Dexamenos from Chios, with a profile of a bearded, large-jawed man (fig. 50) is a particularly strong instance of a "portrait." Chios was part of East Greece, where there were many Greek artists in the service of the Persian governors. Since the early fourth century they cut surprisingly individual likenesses of their masters on coin dies, where Pharnabassos, Tissaphernes, and other figures known from the pages of history are shown with some distinguishing characteristics. It should be recalled, however, that the Greek artisans undoubtedly ennobled these portraits and that the coin images fall basically inside the category of barbarians, well-established in Greek art. Also from the first half of the fourth century are several images of fierce old men on the electrum staters of Kyzikos (fig. 41). The engraver must have learned from Demetrios of Alopeke.

Figure 48. *Lysimache (?) Roman marble copy after a bronze statue by Demetrios of Alopeke erected on the Acropolis in the early fourth century B.C. London, British Museum.*

Figure 49. *Corinthian general (Pelichos?), inscribed (secondarily) as Archidamos. Roman marble herm from the Villa dei Papiri after a bronze original by Demetrios of Alopeke from the early fourth century B.C. Naples, National Museum.*

Figure 50. *Bearded man. Gem signed by Dexamenos. Late fifth century B.C. Boston, Museum of Fine Arts.*

fig. 51

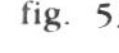

fig. 52

fig. 53

Figure 51. *Electrum stater of Kyzikos. Early fourth century B.C. Istanbul, Archaeological Museum.*

Figure 52. *Plato. Roman marble head after a bronze statue by Silanion set up in the Academy after 347 B.C. Private collection.*

Figure 53. *Bearded man from an Attic grave relief. Ca. 340 B.C. Copenhagen, Ny Carlsberg Glyptotek.*

The first wave of Greek portraits broke away from the perfect beauty of the classical type to create an image of the individual, but their characteristics remained on the exterior. The first version of Socrates' portrait (fig. 46 above) illustrates both points well. The second third of the fourth century brought a new conception of portraiture, with serious attempts at psychological insight and the rendering of emotions. A representative of this trend was the sculpture Silanion. The historical sources mention several portraits by him, but only one has been securely identified, his Plato (fig. 52, see also no. 9). The statue of Plato must have been erected in the Academy just after his death in 347, dedicated by Mithridates, a noble Persian who was a student of the philosopher. Plato was represented seated, immersed in the world of his ideas. Despite their reputation, his philosophical ideas do not lend him a joyful appearance. On close analysis the character remains more general than individual: Plato is shown as a type of thinker, modifying the appearance of the man to suit the image rather than suggesting a unique physiognomy.

In spite of this modest degree of "realism," there is much that is purely ideal in Plato's portrait. Any direct expression of his age—over eighty—is avoided. He is depicted as if he still had all his teeth; one could innocently proclaim that Plato preserved his, but other aged men are portrayed in the same way at this time. One could say that the portrait is an idea of Plato much more than Plato himself. Plato's image has been used to provide general characteristics for other people on several Attic grave monuments from the third quarter of the century (fig. 53). It would be naive to suppose that various unknown Athenians actually looked like Plato (or later like Aristotle). Thus a face connected with a famous name was used in this way to designate "character" as described later by Aristotle's follower Theophrastos in a work called *Charakteres*. People aspired less to be presented as ideal, impersonal citizens than they desired to be shown corresponding with certain standard types with marked social status: thinker, orator, statesman, dreamer, or even man prone to anger. With this development we are on the way to the four basic types of human nature, the representatives of the four humours which would dominate the characterology of portraiture until the nineteenth century.

Other portraits can be attributed to Silanion. Miltiades, the victorious commander at Marathon, appears in a highly impersonal image (fig. 54 reproduces the uninscribed herm in Ravenna, as the face of the inscribed one in the same museum was heavily restored in the second half of the sixteenth century), perhaps a reshaping of the Pheidian statue in Delphi. Another unknown philosopher of Silanion's style figures in the Getty Museum collection (no. 5). Many others could be mentioned, among them the portrait identified as Herakleitos. Also the excellent portrait of Thucydides (no. 7) belongs to the same circle. As Thucydides died at the beginning of the fourth century, his portrait must be a retrospective one. More than half a century later,

fig. 54

fig. 55

fig. 56

fig. 57

the image of the greatest historian was revised to seem apparently more personal (no. 8). He is older and more preoccupied, more *gravis*. Thucydides appears in the second version as the judge of the history he lived. An excellent bronze statuette (in the Cabinet des Médailles, Bibliothèque Nationale) shows the seated figure with an expressive head and a pointing gesture (fig. 55) presenting his work as a treasure for all times—*ktema es aei*.

After the disaster at Chaironeia in 338, the Athenian democracy with unusual commonsense voted for Lykourgus as administrator of public finances for many consecutive years. Lykourgus was a man of outstanding managerial talent and probity. He succeeded in creating a surplus budget and was able to complete an extensive building program second only to the vast Periklean enterprises of the previous century. Among his accomplishments is the theater of Dionysos, which was rebuilt and redecorated with statues representing famous men of the past. These included the classics of the theater, the three princes of tragedy—Aischylos, Sophokles, and Euripides—and the naughty but gracious child of the Muses, the comedian Aristophanes, all represented standing. There is also a good possibility that more memorials were erected in the theater at the same time. Two of them, honoring Miltiades and Themistokles, can be traced partially on Roman coins. The Sophokles has survived in a full size statue (fig. 56)—a portly man, graciously enveloping his bulk in a himation with a characteristic mild expression on his visage, radiating a well-balanced wisdom and sense of deep poetry. Some knowledge of Sophokles' actual appearance must have been available to the artist. Later, perhaps only in the second century B.C., a new version of Sophokles was created (see no. 52), one that enhanced the signs of very old age to the detriment of the quiet equanimity.

The classical period of the fourth century proceeded differently. As we can see from the Roman copies surviving of the head of Aischylos (fig. 57), there was no historical memory on which the artist could base his likeness. The sculptor essentially added age, a long beard, and some other minor variations to the Sophokles type. The result is that Aischylos seems less individual than Sophokles, but in his old age he looks venerable,

Figure 54. *Miltiades. Roman marble herm after a bronze statue from the third quarter of the fourth century B.C. Ravenna, National Museum.*

Figure 55. *Thucydides. Roman bronze statuette after a Greek original. Paris, Cabinet des Médailles.*

Figure 56. *Sophokles. Roman marble copy after the bronze statue set up in the theater of Dionysos in Athens in the 30s of the fourth century B.C. Vatican.*

Figure 57. *Aischylos. Roman marble head after a Greek bronze statue set up in the theater of Dionysos in Athens in the 30s of the fourth century B.C. Naples, National Museum.*

Figure 58. *Euripides. Roman marble herm after a Greek bronze statue set up in the theater of Dionysos in Athens in the 30s of the fourth century B.C. Copenhagen, Ny Carlsberg Glyptotek.*

Figure 59. *Euripides. Roman inscribed marble head after a bronze statue by Lysippos from the 30s of the fourth century B.C. Naples, National Museum.*

Figure 60. *Alexander the Great. Marble head connected with the work of Leochares. Ca. 338 B.C. Athens, Acropolis Museum.*

not decrepit. Some archaeologists think the corresponding statue of Aischylos may survive in a marble copy which shows the mantle around the hips and a rather youthful naked upper body. The head of Euripides from the group (fig. 58) has been identified by a quotation from one of his tragedies incised on a herm replica. He seems to be made in imitation of another excellent portrait of Euripides (fig. 59, see also no. 15), that shows a pessimist who has lost his teeth but not his vulnerability towards the bittersweet indifference of things. While the three standing playwrights in the theater of Dionysos may have been commissioned from Leochares, there was a seated statue, another Euripides, rightly attributed to Lysippos. Lysippos and Leochares worked together in the very late fourth century on an elaborate monument dedicated to Philip and Alexander at Olympia. It is a great pity that no direct trace of this work survives; it would be interesting to see how such different temperaments, Leochares the traditionalist and Lysippos the innovator, could mix.

From the psychology of Silanion's portraits, Leochares returned to the paradigm of classical beauty. His youthful Alexander (fig. 60), which can be traced in several copies, must have been commissioned during Alexander's one short stay in Athens, when the prince escorted back the Athenian prisoners taken at Chaironeia (338 B.C.). This portrait, with considerable elaboration of the hair, also served as the basis for the rejuvenated posthumous images of Alexander (see also no. 19). The Philip attributed to Leochares is identified in numerous replicas, including one in the Getty Museum (no. 4) that was carved with a mild depersonalized elegance. One of the Roman copies found in the Villa dei Papiri has a large, twisted diadem on the head, an ornament of Persian origin which indicates the father's intentions for conquest realized only by the son. A portrait of a strategos (no. 7) with features comparable to Philip's and dated to the third quarter of the fourth century may be added to the *oeuvre* of Leochares.

fig. 61

fig. 62

fig. 63

The young Lysippos may have created portraits before the middle of the fourth century, but we can only follow his work from later in his life with the Euripides done in the early 30s (see fig. 59), the Aristotle dedicated by Alexander in Athens (no. 12 and fig. 63 below) and the second type of Socrates also cast for Athens (see fig. 47 above). The last is a glorious evocation of the master, but the Aristotle is often called the first "real" Greek protrait.

A late epigram praises the very old Lysippos for having set the image of Aesop in front of the portraits on the Seven Wise Men. The Lysippic Aesop may perhaps have been recognized in an expressive head (see p. 37 and fig. 87). This may or may not imply that he was also responsible for the seven statues. The heads of several of the Seven Wise Men survive in various copies, and there are also small seated full figure versions. Can we interpret Aesop as standing in front of the Seven? At least our identification of Lysippos' head of Aesop (see pp. 36–37 below) points to a standing statue. Not all of the Seven Wise Men are Lysippic in style, but there were several traditions about them. There are more than enough colleagues for the college of Seven from antiquity and different, sometimes local, traditions for their statues. The series associated with Lysippos seems to include the candidates chosen by Demetrios of Phaleron, who was first a student of Aristotle's school (under Theophrastos) and then for some ten years dictator of Athens by the grace of the Macedonian king Kassandros. In his old age he was chief librarian for King Ptolemy of Egypt. Probably in this last period of his life he published a compendium on the Seven Wise Men, including a collection of their famous sayings. He also edited the Aesopic fables. It would be tempting to suppose that Demetrios commissioned Lysippos (who was also in Macedonian service) to carve the seven portraits and Aesop (fig. 87). The surviving Periander (no. 17) has been frequently compared with Aristotle, supporting the attribution to Lysippos. In general, the seven are less personal than the animated and well-characterized Aesop. Lysippos' Socrates may have been commissioned by Demetrios of Phaleron too. He may have been thinking about his own role: already Plato had proposed philosophers as city rulers.

The last portrait by Lysippos mentioned by the historical sources is the portrait of Seleukos, one of the successors of Alexander. The piece was apparently labeled "king" by the inscription, a title Seleukos took only in 306 B.C., but this may have been a later addition to an earlier monument. If a bronze head from the Villa dei Papiri (fig. 61) is a Roman reproduction of this portrait, then this must have been created very late in Lysippos' career since Seleukos appears very aged. This brilliantly characterized portrait, as has been poetically observed, resembles Goethe in his last years. A new proposition may be mentioned here: a hitherto unknown portrait of Philip, father of Alexander, by Lysippos (fig. 62). The identity is established by a small carved ivory found in a grave supposed to be Philip's, which alludes even to the fact that Philip was missing an eye. The attribution to Lysippos is confirmed by comparison with his Aristotle.

Figure 61. *Seleukos. Roman bronze head from the Villa dei Papiri, perhaps after a work by Lysippos from the end of the fourth century B.C. Naples, National Museum.*

Figure 62. *Philip II. Roman marble head after a bronze statue by Lysippos from the 30s of the fourth century B.C. Florence, Palazzo Riccardi.*

Figure 63. *Aristotle. Roman marble head after a statue by Lysippos from about 430 B.C. Vienna, Kunsthistorisches Museum.*

fig. 64

fig. 65

fig. 66

Figure 64. *Azara Alexander. Roman marble herm from Hadrian's Villa after a bronze statue by Lysippos from about 330 B.C. Paris, Louvre.*

Figure 65. *Alexander with the Lance. Roman bronze statuette after the famous work of Lysippos from after 330 B.C. Paris, Louvre.*

Figure 66. *Demetrios Poliorketes. Roman marble herm from the Villa dei Papiri after a statue by Teisikrates from about 300 B.C. Naples National Museum.*

ALEXANDER, HIS FOLLOWERS, AND HELLENISTIC PORTRAITS

Lysippos's most notable invention in portraiture resulted from his relationship with Alexander. The literary tradition relates, with some exaggeration, that Alexander refused to be portrayed by anyone by Lysippos. The best version of Lysippos' Alexander seems to be preserved in a poor, academic herm reduction known in two examples from Hadrian's Villa at Tivoli. The better one was presented to Napoleon by his Spanish admirer Nicolas Azara (fig. 64); the other, a complete ruin, is also in the Louvre. The face, comparable in proportions to the Apoxyomenos, the Athlete-Scraper by Lysippos, elevates the traditional perfection of classic beauty to direct apotheosis, enhanced by the *anastole* (the hair fluffed into a leonine mane). Lysippos also gave Alexander *hygrotes*, the moist look in the eye, taken over from representations of Aphrodite, where it designated her irresistible attractiveness. For Alexander the *hygrotes* showed the divine inspiration of the irresistible conqueror.

Of the many other representations of Alexander by Lysippos, the most famous was the Alexander with the Lance, a revolutionary work which opened the traditional closing contours of Greek statues with a fiery gesture and a heavenward-gazing head. This famous statue is best preserved in a poorly conserved bronze statuette in the Louvre (fig. 65). There are some later variants of the Alexander with the Lance, including a rather good late Hellenistic marble statuette in the Getty Museum (no. 21). Thus Lysippos introduced in Greek portraiture a completely new category—the image of the superhuman ruler—an image continued and perfected in the Hellenistic period, one which continually inspired the Romans.

Lysippos' immediate followers in his own school at first turned back to a kind of artificial classicism, perhaps because the changes introduced by the master were too strong. Teisikrates from Sikyon produced a portrait of Demetrios Poliorketes—the most Alexander-like of Alexander's successors, whose defeat at Ipsos in 301 ended the hope of maintaining the unity of Alexander's empire. The similarity to Alexander is easy to detect with the *anastole*, the heaven-gazing pose, and the youthfully idealized face. The whole conception of the portrait, including the little bull's horns—an allusion to a theriomorphic deity—helped to assure the identification of the outstanding but not necessarily faithful marble replica in the Villa dei Papiri (fig. 66, compare also no. 27). Some other related heads add little to a rather conventionalized image of a ruler who in his youth may have looked perhaps like the blossoming ephebic athlete of the Getty Bronze—a work by Lysippos himself (no. 25).

fig. 67

fig. 68

fig. 69

fig. 70

The different trends of ruler portraits in the Hellenistic period correspond mostly to geographical regions. Sculpture in Alexandria was nourished on the style of Praxiteles, with an added emphasis on soft modeling and sfumato of the surface. But the portraits of the Ptolemies themselves are typified by a brutal realism, cruelly revealing the progressive degeneration of the dynasty. This is especially true for the male members of the dynasty; their sister-wives remain for the most part ideally beautiful, even if some personal elements mark their features (fig. 67). The identification of the early Ptolemies is often difficult because they were depicted intentionally similar. The coins are only of limited help in fitting names to faces. The distinguishing of one Ptolemy from another is still more difficult among the traditional representations of them as Egyptian pharaohs (see no. 32). The bodies are completely Egyptian while in the heads an infiltration of Greek elements is perceptible. Yet even here some individualization can be detected. A possible Ptolemy the Second in the Getty collection (no. 28) comes from Asia Minor. Its style modifies the Hellenistic koine with Alexandrian soft modeling. While there was hardly any attempt to flatter the man, the piece does show a preoccupation with enhancing the apotheosis of a ruler. Probably after his death, the original hair on the piece was cut down to accomodate a helmet in the shape of an elephant's head, a helmet style Alexander is known to have worn on statues. Two deep cavities were cut in to support the tusks.

Another case of refurbishing the headdress of a Hellenistic head, also from Asia Minor, is the supposed Attalos I from Pergamon (figs. 68–69). Its originally modest hair style was cut down after the ruler's death and replaced by an overwhelming wig, which gives the sitter a more superhuman appearance. Another portrait, in the J. Paul Getty Museum, probably of a Seleucid ruler, represents another version of the Baroque trend in Hellenistic sculpture (no. 33) on the edge of the Greek world, the far northeast of Alexander's empire. The portraits of the Bactrian kingdom (approximately today's Afghanistan) reach the most strikingly realistic treatment. The faces are so defined by age and ravaged by experience that one could think of them as ancestors of the Roman emperor Vespasian who chose to be shown like an old, shrewd, toothless farmer.

From the end of the second century B.C., the portraits of Hellenistic rulers served as models for the images of victorious Roman generals. The affinity between them is sometimes so close that archaeologists hesitate about the dates and identities. One of the distinctive features of Hellenistic princes is the royal taenia, always worn (even on monetary portraits) by Hellenistic rulers. It would have been the height of impropriety for a Roman citizen to wear one. That is why the so-called Sulla (fig. 70) in the Getty Museum, which shows a revival of Lysippic proportions and the ethos of a Hellenistic conqueror, must be a Roman.

Figure 67. *Arsinoe II (ca. 316–270 B.C.) Boston, Museum of Fine Arts.*

Figure 68/ 69. *Marble head of a Hellenistic ruler from Pergamon. Early second century B.C. East Berlin, Pergamon Museum. Figure 68: original appearance. Figure 69: with posthumously added hair.*

Figure 70. *So-called Sulla. Bronze portrait head of a Roman from the early first century B.C. Malibu, The J. Paul Getty Museum.*

fig. 71

fig. 72

fig. 73

fig. 74

Figure 71. ***Athenian statesman. Roman marble head after an early third century B.C. original. Kassel, Museum.***

Figure 72. ***Theophrastos. Roman marble head after an original from the beginning of the third century B.C. Rome, Capitoline Museum.***

Figure 73. ***Epicurus. Roman marble head after an Attic original from the first half of the third century B.C. New York, The Metropolitan Museum of Art.***

Figure 74. ***Chrysippos. Roman marble statue (with plaster cast of a marble head in the British Museum) after an Attic original by Timarchides set up in the Kerameikos at the end of the third century B.C. Paris, Louvre.***

The images of rulers constitute only one part of Hellenistic portraiture. There was a continuation and multiplication of the monuments for famous men of the past and an inflation of honorary statues for real or supposed benefactors of cities. In third century Athern two parallel and convergent lines of development can be traced. The first continues the classical tradition of the fourth century. The best example of this is the effigy of the comic poet Menander (no. 34), erected as a seated statue in the Athenian Agora. The preserved base of the statue names as sculptors Kephisodotos and Timarchos the Younger, sons of the great Praxiteles. They must have learned much from Lysippos, especially in the elaborate modeling of the hair, but the presentation of the personality and the structure of the rather big head remain in the Attic tradition. Another portrait (fig. 71), perhaps earlier, uses the same hairstyle, and the original must have been created by the same hand. It may represent an Athenian politician from the turn of the century, well considered by his city as one replica is coupled with Miltiades in a double herm in the Prado. The man must have had some relationship with Menander; their personalities are rendered in a similar way and they wear the same elaborate hair style. The portraits must have been created by the same sculptor.

The portrait of Theophrastos (fig. 72), successor of Aristotle in the Lyceum, represents an opposite conception. His unflattering visage points to the images of Demosthenes (no. 40) and Phokion (no. 41). The impressive portrait study of Demosthenes was erected in the Agora in 280 B.C. and sculpted by Polyeuktos. The portraits of the three Epicureans represent a further development of this "noble," more classical line of portraiture. Chronologically they range from 277 B.C., when Epicurus himself ordered the statue of his beloved pupil Metrodoros (fig. 83) to the middle of the century, the date of the statue erected to the memory of Hermarchos, the successor to Epicurus as director of the school. Epicurus's own image (fig. 72) (see nos. 37 and 38) of circa 270 is the strongest of the three, and one of the most impressive of all Greek portraits. The two students, in comparison, appear more classical, perhaps only because Epicurus was such an imposing personality.

The other trend in portraiture at this time is represented by the effigies of the Stoicians. Zeno (no. 49) and his student and follower Kleanthes (no. 50) share an association with the same school of philosophy but also a common ethnic origin. However, Kleanthes is shown looking less anxious and tense than his master. The next major Stoic teacher, Chrysippos, who really spread the teachings of his school, was portrayed at the very end of the century by Timarchides, member of a family of reputed sculptors. The realism of Chrysippos' face (fig. 74) is very detailed and descriptive. Even though the psychological penetration is very deep, the artist was concerned first with recording every little sign of Chrysippos' old age. One could say that the sitter must have had many sleepless nights. The portrait, which may possibly represent Hippokrates (no. 51), the

fig. 75

fig. 76

fig. 77

Figure 75. *Old Fisherman. Detail of a Roman marble statue after an original from the late third century B.C. Vatican.*

Figure 76. *Homer. Roman marble head after a Hellenistic statue from the second/first century B.C. Paris, Louvre.*

Figure 77. *Karneades. Roman marble head after a Hellenistic statue.*

father of medicine who lived in the earlier fifth century, is so like the image of Chrysippos that the attribution of both portraits to the same hand is evident.

The "leaders" of another philosophical school, the Cynics, appeared next in time. Krates, second in line after Antisthenes, is usually considered to have had his portrait (no. 44) made at the same time as Plato. But Plato's image is only quoted in this image, and the portrait of Kratippos must have been carved more than one century posthumously. The same is true for the Baroque image of the founder of the Cynics, Antisthenes (no. 45). His portrait was formerly dated to the fourth century, a generation after his lifetime. An inscription found several years ago in Ostia proves, however, that Antisthenes' well-documented image was carved by Phyromachos, champion of the Hellenistic Baroque around 200 B.C. As with Kratippos, the superficial resemblance to Plato is purely a result of the artist's conscious quotation of Plato's well-known portrait. The long beard and hair of Antisthenes not only identify him as philosopher but also show how free he was of any social constraints; they also result from the artist's joy in the sharp movement of light and shadow in the deeply undercut hair framing the face. Perhaps most reputed of the Cynics was the self-proclaimed beggar Diogenes, who ostensibly chose to live a life free from any worldly goods. His portrait was rendered by a sculptor who brilliantly turned the pathos of high Hellenistic portraiture into genre (no. 46). The clearest expression of it is in relief representations (no. 47) of the ragged philosopher inside his barrel home, with his begging bag and a faithful mongrel dog. Even in replicas of the head alone, the philosopher appears as the first hobo; the Getty Museum head (no. 46) is of rather outstanding quality.

The second century B.C. saw in its first half the peak of the Hellenistic Baroque art. At least two of the portraits in the Getty Museum belong to this period, both showing agitated old men, a poet (no. 43) and a philosopher (no. 6). This is also the period to which belongs a portrait that was extremely popular in antiquity and famous in modern times, since the Renaissance when it acquired the name of Seneca (fig. 86). It shows a non-Greek face in a moment of anxiety, its ugly features converted to an image of appealing spirituality. It is evident that in spite of all the realism and the characterization no real person was depicted. It is a typical imaginary portrait, one of the *non traditii vultus*—a famous man of the past whose real features were not preserved. Pseudo-Seneca is probably Aesop, the fabulist, who became himself the subject of a fable (see pp. 37–38 for the arguments in favor of the identification). Reconstructed portraits existed from the beginning of the classical age, starting with the first portrait of Homer through, for example, the Seven Wise Men created by Lysippos. Most of them are basically ideal heads with the addition of some appropriate characteristics based on the literary record or borrowed from an analogous portrait. The extreme case is probably the portrait of Hippokrates (see also no. 51). But the reconstructions made later in the

fig. 78

fig. 79

Figure 78. ***Poseidonios. Roman marble head after a first century B.C. statue. Naples, National Museum.***

Figure 79. ***Bronze portrait head found in Delos. Ca. 100 B.C. Athens, National Museum.***

Hellenistic period, including the Pseudo-Seneca, were created differently. Their point of departure is genre representation, the type of work well known in such popular statues as the Old Fisherman (fig. 75). The same category of genre served also as the major inspiration for the ravaged faces of venerable senators in the Roman Republic.

Another imaginary portrait dates from this time and this stylistic trend. It is not only the most impressive among Greek portraits but is also perhaps the greatest portrait of all time—the Blind Homer (fig. 76). Contrary to the elevated classical image of the poet (fig. 35), this is a merciless portrayal of decrepit old age and a man handicapped by blindness. In the end it is also the apotheosis of spirit in the exuberant creation over the relentless decay of the flesh. The bones of the face poke through the atrophying muscles and sagging flesh. The crown of the hair is like an artificial addition. The lips are sunk in the patriarchal beard. But above all are the eyes, with pouches below them and cruelly extinct vision, behind whose dark curtain are the powerful flames of his second sight: the holy city of Priam burning, the heroes falling in the dust, the immortal horses neighing, the black ships avoiding the monsters emerging from the violet sea, and over all, the sunny heaven of Hellas like the smile of Golden Aphrodite. There is no external evidence to identify the portrait as Homer, but since its "rediscovery" in the late fifteenth century it has been universally accepted as him. It should be noted that the date of the original is disputed. The suffering Laocoon which is the nearest kin in artistic expression has been given vacillating dates between the second and the first centuries B.C.

By the middle of the second century, an artificial return to classical models pervaded all Greek art, affecting portraits too. Of the numerous portraits from this time, the head of Karneades (fig. 77), a distant follower of Plato, may be mentioned for the second century, and Poseidonios (fig. 78) who taught the Romans Stoic philosophy, for the first century. The characterization in both is subtle and the sculpture correct, but the results are increasingly dry and "academic." This is the neoclassical trend that the Romans were to adopt in the later first century B.C., though at first they favored the other, more Baroque trend. Both styles existed simultaneously, a phenomenon which can be compared to the acceptance of parallel styles of rhetoric in the golden age of public speaking, the last century of the Republic: the Asianic and the Attic. But even at the close of Greek portraiture, excellent works were produced. Surviving testimony to this is an astonishing bronze original, the head found on the island of Delos (fig. 79) which depicts a mature man. His face communicates such a complex human being that he could also be a fellow of our times.

fig. 80 fig. 80

Figure 80. *Roman marble herm from the Villa dei Papiri, inscribed "Panyassis." Naples, National Museum.*

GREEK PORTRAITS AMONG THE GREEKS

Something general should be said about the presentation of Greek portraits. Throughout Greek history, as illustrated in the survey above, they were public monuments. They were full-length, usually over lifesize statues showing the complete body in a characteristic pose or even a dramatic situation. Like the portrait head, the body and pose were individualized to some extent, perhaps especially to the sensitive classical Greek eye. Thus the Tyrant Slayers (figs. 25–28) were shown side by side accomplishing their deed. They were not an active sculptural group as the nineteenth century would understand one; the slain tyrant is, is, of course, not represented. The statue group showed their glorious action; it was not a vulgar *tableau vivant*. The action is not consummated but indicated in a Greek way. Demosthenes (no. 40) was represented standing as an orator; he is not shown addressing the assembly but rather with the thoughts for his speech going through his head. Chrysippos (fig. 74) was represented seated with one hand extended toward his audience and a finger pointed upward to emphasize a single argument of his pedagogical demonstration. Usually a statesman or war captain is shown standing. On the other hand, philosophers are mostly seated, although Cynic philosophers are shown standing, while the most famous of them—Diogenes—is shown, at least in reliefs, with the barrel in which he lived. Socrates was represented both ways. Most poets also stand in the act of singing their verse. While the three dramatic poets—Aischylos, Sophokles, Euripides—erected by the statesman Lykourgus in the 330s in the theater of Athens were standing, the Lysippic version of Euripides was surely seated. In general there are standard, well-defined types for poets and philosophers. The poets often have a fillet of wool around the head, but the indication continues in the "character" of the face. There is even something like a type of Epicurean philosopher as opposed to a type of Stoic philosopher.

There are practically no originals of Greek portraits that survive, and Roman copies preserve few of the full-length statues. Conforming to their traditional preference, the Romans conceived of personality as limited to the head and face. Copying Greek classics, most of the Roman craftsmen proceeded carefully but without any impetus to be creative, cautiously preserving not only the number and direction of individual locks of hair but also the inclination of the head and neck from a Greek statue. Thus from most of the Roman replicas of heads we can determine whether the original statue was standing or seated. Herms sometimes even give a limited idea of the whole body.

Most Roman copies are marble; a few of them are in bronze. One might expect the bronze copies to be more faithful, as they could have been cast directly from the originals. The majority of Greek originals were bronzes, mounted in bases that usually gave the name of the person represented; an appropriate verse praising his merits, especially if the statue were a public dedication; the name of the dedicant; and the signature of the sculptor. Other appropriate features were sometimes added, especially in Roman copies, like a quotation from the subject's work. Some original bases survive (mentioned above: Perikles, Lysimache, Menander). A tiny chip from the inscribed base of the Tyrant Slayers was found in the American excavations of the Athenian Agora.

GREEK PORTRAITS AND ROMAN PATRONS

The Romans made copies of Greek sculpture in general, but the portraits are a special category. The statues of gods and heroes attracted them because they were famous art, because they provided decoration for architectural settings, and, in the case of cult statues, because of the subjects. Greek portraits, on the contrary, reflect the Roman claim to be the heirs of Greek culture. They established the notorious or famous figures of Greek politicians, philosophers, and poets as "classics." The copies were made both by public initiative and for private houses. We hear already in Republican times that, following the recommendation of an oracle, the magistrates erected in the Roman Forum the statues of Pythagoras, the wisest of the Greeks, and of Alkibiades, the most courageous of them. Cicero exhibited in his villa a portrait of Plato to demonstrate to visitors that he claimed his philosophical ancestry from attending classes at the Academy, which in his day continued the tradition of Plato's school, at least in its location. His friend Atticus, of a more pragmatic nature, fostered an image of Aristotle in his home. Both in modest houses in Pompeii and in the luxurious villas of Herculaneum we find portraits of Greek classics. The copies are mostly of inexpensive marble. Bronze copies are rare and not necessarily very good.

First one basic fact has to be stated. The original Greek portraits were public monuments; thus, they were complete statues. The Romans insisted, as with their own portraits, mostly on heads. The standard form of the Roman portrait is the bust, but rarely, except in some small bronzes, is the shape of the Roman bust ever used for a Greek classic. Instead the Romans, perhaps following the late Hellenistic models, used herms—prismatic pillars—complete with indication of sex and geometric square protuberances instead of arms.

Roman public places, especially libraries, often exhibited real "galleries" of Greek portraits, summarizing what they considered as important in the Greek heritage. The best known ensemble was erected by the emperor Hadrian in his villa at Tivoli. Unfortunately, of his extensive collection, mostly inscribed pillars survive without their heads. Thus, for example, for Pheidias we have just the bottom of such a pillar with the inscription and feet. Private houses boasted smaller groups, often reflecting the philosophical inclinations of the owner; thus in the Villa dei Papiri the owner had at least three galleries, one a set of marble herms that remains enigmatic since the copies were not executed in the standard mechanical three-point technique but were made freehand. Consequently some identifications have been proposed but none of them have received general agreement. In two cases, where there are traces of a hand-written inscription, the resulting identifications are clearly spurious (see also pp. 33–34). A series of large bronze heads, including Seleukos

fig. 81

Figure 81. *Marble head of "Parmenides" found in Elea. Velia, Antiquario.*

(fig. 61) is from the second gallery. But there is another one of small bronze portrait busts with inscriptions which provided definitive identifications of Demosthenes, Zeno, and confirmed Epicurus. A fourth man, surely a philospher, remains anonymous. This is perhaps a good opportunity to look at the meaning of this assemblage. The reason for Epicurus is clear: the large library which gave the name to the Villa dei Papiri contained mostly Epicurean texts. But what about Zeno the Stoic and the great orator and patriot Demosthenes? They were at least equally popular in Roman times if one considers the number of replicas. The modest galleries from two houses in Pompeii, probably more characteristic for common Roman taste, present equally disparate compositions. One contains Epicurus, Seneca, and Demosthenes; the other, Pseudo-Seneca and Epicurus. Perhaps the explanation for the seemingly random grouping may be as follows: Epicurus corresponds to the owner's personal belief while Demosthenes, the intrepid fighter for freedom who paid with his own life, may be an unpunishable reflection of Republican political nostalgia against the empire. Pseudo-Seneca, who is perhaps the most common Greek portrait in Roman copies, may reflect the first literary occupation of every man who learned to read: as discussed in more detail below (pp. 36–37), he may be Aesop. Thus even the apparent antagonism of Epicurus and Zeno in the Villa dei Papiri is understandable: the first reflects the personal beliefs of the owner while the Stoic represented an educated man's philosophical cloak for true Roman virtue.

Of course the Romans also liked small portraits in precious materials and still more the reduced portraits of famous Greeks in engraved gems which they wore in rings. There are many images of Epicurus, Demosthenes, and several others, sometimes of outstanding artistic quality. Of course, Roman doctors like Hippocrates (see also no. 51).

Starting in the second century A.D., the Romans began to combine Greek portraits in a new way, this time physically and in pairs: double herms. Two herms are united in a way that the occiputs merge. There are four ears, and the hairstyles cross from one to the other. The meaning of some of these marriages is evident at once: Plato is a natural companion for his master Socrates; Sophokles couples well with Aischylos, and even more frequently with Euripides. In many other instances the interpretation is more difficult, like Homer and Menander. If we do not know the names, the way is open for idle speculation: usually too much common sense and modern logic results in the wrong identifications. However, next to providing an unusual insight into the Roman approach to Greek culture, both double herms and galleries present us with some help for identifications. To turn to the Getty Museum collection, Plato and Aristotle are excellent companions (no. 11), but how can it be explained that Antisthenes, the ranking Cynic philosopher, is coupled with a poet known in other replicas and called either, more probably, Pindar or, more recently, Archilochos (no. 45). It is certain that the join is not an accident; gallery association brings them both together another time (in the British Museum, together with the three Epicureans and Zeno).

fig. 82

Figure 82. *Metrodoros. Roman marble head after a first half of the third century B.C. Attic original. Berlin Museum.*

THE GAME OF THE NAMES

Since the Renaissance the first preoccupation of anyone liking or researching Greek portraits has been, "Who is it?" The search for actual likeness is, of course, vain. The portraits do not show how a famous Greek looked but, rather, how his contemporaries—and in the case of Roman copies, another community—saw him. But the search for identifications has not lost its charm, and he who commits no sins in this connection—including the writer of these lines—may cast the first stone.

The generally established rule is that an inscribed piece gives the most complete guarantee for an identification. Unfortunately, many herm prisms with excellent inscriptions have reached us headless. But there is worse yet: the ancients were even more careless than modern archaeologists, sometimes putting a well-engraved name under a face that surely represents someone else. Some examples: two marble herms from the Villa dei Papiri are provided with inscriptions written in ink but in good, monumental characters. One (fig. 49) gives the name of the Spartan king Archidamos (without a numeral), which has led to discussion of endless possibilities and chronological sequences but seemed basically secure. The other herm's inscription, faded to a great extent, was recently read by a resourceful Italian scholar. The piece (fig. 80) should represent the epic poet Panyassis, uncle of the historian Herodotos, active in the early fifth century B.C. Here the difficulties start: the style of the head points to the late third century B.C. and is not a posthumous fantasy as in the case of Homer; one receives a good impression of a real personality. There is hardly any chance that a tradition of the poet's appearance survived from the early fifth century and was revived later. The inevitable conclusion is that some young participant in the literary and philosophical circle of the Villa dei Papiri, perhaps bored with a text of the old-fashioned poet, put his name on an old bust. It is difficult to identify another replica as the series of marble herms from the Villa dei Papiri were carved freehand.

This discovery, of course, projects some doubts on the Spartan king Archidamos, and in his case also another identity cannot be excluded. The style, even in the freehand interpretation, corresponds to the group of portraits associated with Demetrios of Alopeke. The literary tradition gives Demetrios, among others, an unflattering image as an aging Corinthian strategos, Pelichos, who may have previously been labeled in the Villa "Archidamos," as the herm is a cuirassed warrior. One of two other replicas may exist.

A still more evident case of misidentification is the herm inscribed PARMENIDES (fig. 81) found not long ago in Elea where this philosopher lived in the fifth century B.C. A marble head fits it perfectly, but the face is one more of numerous replicas known without any doubt as Metrodoros (fig. 82), pupil and follower of

fig. 83

fig. 84

Figure 83. ***Aristotle. Renaissance drawing after a lost inscribed bust.***

Figure 84. ***Xanthippos. Roman marble head found in Ephesos after the mid fifth century B.C. original by Pheidias. Selçuk, Museum.***

Epicurus. The type cannot be denied, although archaeologists have used contorted arguments to prove that it is slightly different. The truth is simple. When the patres of Roman Velia of the second century A.D. decided to erect a monument of their own classic, they were faced with the absence of any iconographic tradition. One bearded philosopher being much like another, they bought a head of Metrodoros!

One last example of an inaccurate ancient inscription in the Getty Museum collection (no. 81). A herm with a partially preserved inscription states "Periander/ Corinthian/ Take care of everything." The last line was the motto of the early sixth century B.C. Corinthian tyrant who was later incorporated among the legendary Seven Wise Men. Again, the face is a portrait after life and, still worse, does not correspond to the conventional *Fantasienbildnis* of Periander, which is well-known and securely identified. (A rather mistreated copy even exists in the Getty Museum collection (no. 17).) The head on the inscribed herm does, however, correspond perfectly to other replicas of the portrait representing Aischines, the pro-Macedonian Athenian politician who violently opposed Demosthenes. Evidently the ancients cared about completely reliable iconography much less than we do.

However, the inscribed monuments are still far and away the best evidence. Unfortunately, the coins which are excellent for identifying Roman emperors provide only limited help for identifying famous Greeks. This is partly because the likenesses appear only in Roman times on local coinage of famous men's native cities, propaganda for past glories. The quality of the striking is usually very modest, and often the complete statue was reproduced. But occasionally—especially when we have the head—the coins can help. Thus Chrysippos (fig. 74, c. 280–207 B.C.) and his contemporary, the astronomer Aratos, are depicted on each side of the same coin of the city Soloi in Cyprus, where both were born. Mosaics or mural paintings, even with identifying inscriptions, are seldom of assistance. Sometimes a Renaissance drawing registering a lost inscribed monument can provide decisive evidence. Thus Aristotle was identified on the basis of a Renaissance drawing (fig. 83); and so was Menander, until the appearance of the inscribed miniature bronze bust in the Getty Museum (no.34).

Circumstantial evidence offers the largest field for archaeological speculation. Several examples, starting with the possibilities given by the Getty collection, may be presented. Three, perhaps only partially preserved, galleries are exhibited in the Getty Museum. The first exhibits two poets, identified as such by the fillets, in their hair. One (no. 42) is known in two other replicas; the other (no. 43) is unique. The portraits belong respectively to the early third century B.C. and the first half of the second century; nothing more can be said. A second gallery consists of two philosophers, identified as such only by their general psychological bent and grimace. They both look like constipated professors. Again, for one (no. 5) there are two replicas,

fig. 85

Figure 85. ***Anakreon. Roman marble head after the mid fifth century B.C. original by Pheidias. Rome, Palazzo Altemps.***

ours being far the best; the other (no. 6) is unique. The first portrait belongs to the third quarter of the fourth century B.C., the original of the other to the first half of the second century. The first seems to be more joyful, and his advanced age is hardly perceptible in the deep sunk eyes. The other is frankly toothless; but this distinction belongs almost entirely to the styles of the two different periods. Nothing more can be said. The third gallery offers at least a name. In spite of all peculiarities due to the provincial, unpretentious sculptor, one of the heads carved in Haurân basalt surely represents Aristotle (no. 13), as it corresponds well to the numerous known replicas. The other (no. 14) is unique, evidently a *ritratto d'invenzione* without background in any real physiognomy. As the face gives the impression of a theatrical mask, the name of Thespis, the founder of Greek tragedy in the later sixth century B.C., is tentatively advanced. Statues of him existed in antiquity, and an inscription on a base of the Roman period from the theater of Dionysos in Athens survives. And, of course, Aristotle was and remains the best theoretician of tragedy.

The next case is different, concerning a group of helmeted, bearded men. Some dozen different faces are preserved, mostly in several replicas. Only one identity is sure: Perikles, guaranteed by two inscribed pieces (one of them, fig. 39). On this basis it is generally accepted that the helmeted generals must be Athenian strategoi. Another face among them is usually accepted, without any positive proof, as Konon (see no. 2), who successfully broke the Spartan hegemony in the early fourth century. His statue, erected at public expense in Athens, was only the second such case after the Tyrant Slayers (see p. 10).

Two other attempted identifications can be presented here. As mentioned in the historical survey, there were bronze statues on the Acropolis of the poet Anakreon and his friend the strategos Xanthippos, who won a decisive battle in the Graeco-Persian wars and was the father of Perikles. Perikles was probably the dedicant of the two statues, and Pheidias is generally accepted as the sculptor. Anakreon is well known (fig. 36). One replica of the head is inscribed. Several attempts were made to identify Xanthippos, not one of which is widely accepted; but at least for the head there is any easy solution. Xanthippos was a strategos; thus he should be found among the several heads of strategoi of the fifth century. Only one, of which a new copy is in the Getty Museum (no. 1), corresponds well with the replicas of Anakreon, not only in the treatment of the bushy hair and beard but also in the wide open eyes and general appearance.

fig. 86

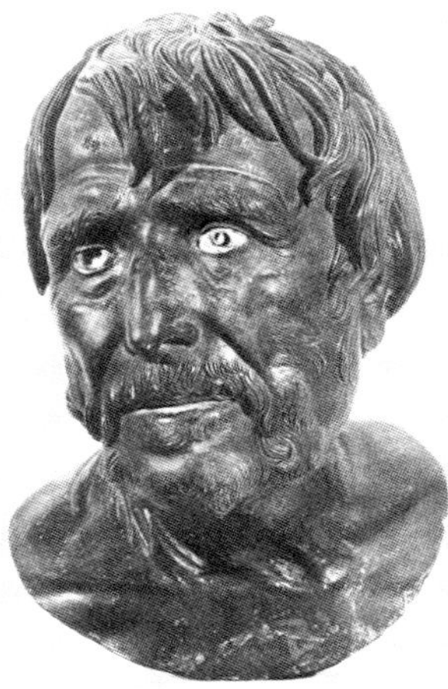

Figure 86. ***Aesop** (so-called Pseudo-Seneca). **Roman bronze head found in the Villa dei Papiri after a mid second century B.C. original. Naples, National Museum.***

Another strategos who may be mentioned here was Phokion. A stern conservative, disciplined soldier, he was the unwilling commander at Chaironeia, the last battle for Greek freedom. He performed his duty brilliantly together with the Theban allies, but nothing could resist the elan of the young Alexander and the military genius of Philip II. The resentful Athenians condemned the old general to death, but some years later had his statue erected in repentance. The man was a contemporary of Demosthenes and shared his destiny; thus from the latest strategoi there is one who can be well compared with Demosthenes for style and expression. Again, the most striking feature is the beard and hair in flat, sparse locks. Until this time only one replica was known, not very good and severely recut. The Getty collection acquired a fragment (no. 41) with the acquiline nose preserved and of excellent carving. The identity seems sure enough, and from now on the fierce likeness of Demosthenes (no. 40) can be confronted with the resigned countenance of the adversary he respected.

Another identification may be attempted for another Greek portrait in the Getty Museum (no. 50). The same bearded philosopher is known in two other replicas, one in Madrid and the other in Leningrad. The portrait has been dated sometime in the fifth century B.C., which is clearly untenable; the face is clearly from the well-advanced third century. Zeno, the Stoic (no. 49), also represented by a well-known collection, is its nearest kin. The affinity includes not only the physical characteristics, possibly ethnic—both men may be Levantine—but also the general mood, which corresponds well to the "character" of a philosopher. The same slightly ascetic tension appears in a completely different face, namely Chrysippos (fig. 74). The spirit and ardor militate against the flesh and the despicable world in general. This settles the identity as a member of the Stoic school, and the ethnic relationship with Zeno means he must be Kleanthes, Zeno's student and successor as head of the school.

fig. 87

Figure 87. ***Aesop. Roman marble head after a statue by Lysippos from the late fourth century B.C. Vatican.***

The last example has no foothold in our collection but concerns perhaps the most famous Greek portrait of all, known in some fifty replicas and countless imitations (fig. 86). The best example is the splendid bronze head from the Villa dei Papiri. The face has been famous since Renaissance times when it acquired the name of Seneca, the Roman orator and poet who became Nero's tutor. Some twenty other names have been proposed by modern archaeologists, none of them with any positive roots. The most frequent were Aristophanes, the Athenian comic poet from the late fifth century, and Hesiod, common already in antiquity as a counterpart of Homer. One of the replicas has an ivy wreath, a good symbol for a poet, and another was found in a theater, thus also good for a poet. But neither Hesiod nor Aristophanes were well-known in Roman times beyond the scholarly interest of professional philologists. Pseudo-Seneca appears coupled in double herms with Menander and another Hellenistic, probably comic, poet. In galleries, he appears with Demosthenes, Epicurus, and also in the large ensemble of the Villa dei Papiri. He evidently made a good counterpart to any classic, but this does not aid a precise identification. The original is generally accepted as a work of the early second century B.C. It is not a real face; the features look much more like a genre creation, comparable, say, to the Old Fisherman (fig. 75), than to a well-defined likeness. The man is not a Greek either. The pattern of classical proportions is abandoned for an utterly rustic, rather barbarian countenance, and the expression shows fear and anxiety. One could say the man is scared to death, which may indeed be imminent. The head is sunk between the shoulders, and the man must have had difficulty in breathing, caused not by emotions but rather by physical deformity. All these characteristics, including the presence of the man only in Roman contexts, correspond well to the half-mythical figure Aesop, who was a barbarian by origin and a slave by social condition. The uncowed teller of short fables reflecting a wisdom unpleasant to Homeric gods and even contemporary Greeks, Aesop is said to have irritated the powerful Delphic clergy so much that a precious gold vessel was slipped in his modest baggage to trap him and condemn him to death. But the reputation of the man remained high. His fables were the first texts read by every Greek and Roman child—the beginning of universal literacy. Later, waiting in prison for his own execution, Socrates put them into verses. The identification of Pseudo-Seneca as Aesop has already been suggested, but these detailed arguments are new. Finally the Pseudo-Seneca may be well compared with an earlier portrait, which may be proposed as the image of Aesop created by Lysippos (fig. 87).

1

1. Xanthippos

After a bronze original by Pheidias, dedicated about the middle of the fifth century on the Acropolis by Perikles. The bushy beard and the expressive eyes are second century A.D. interpretations of the still Severe style original.

1

fig. 88

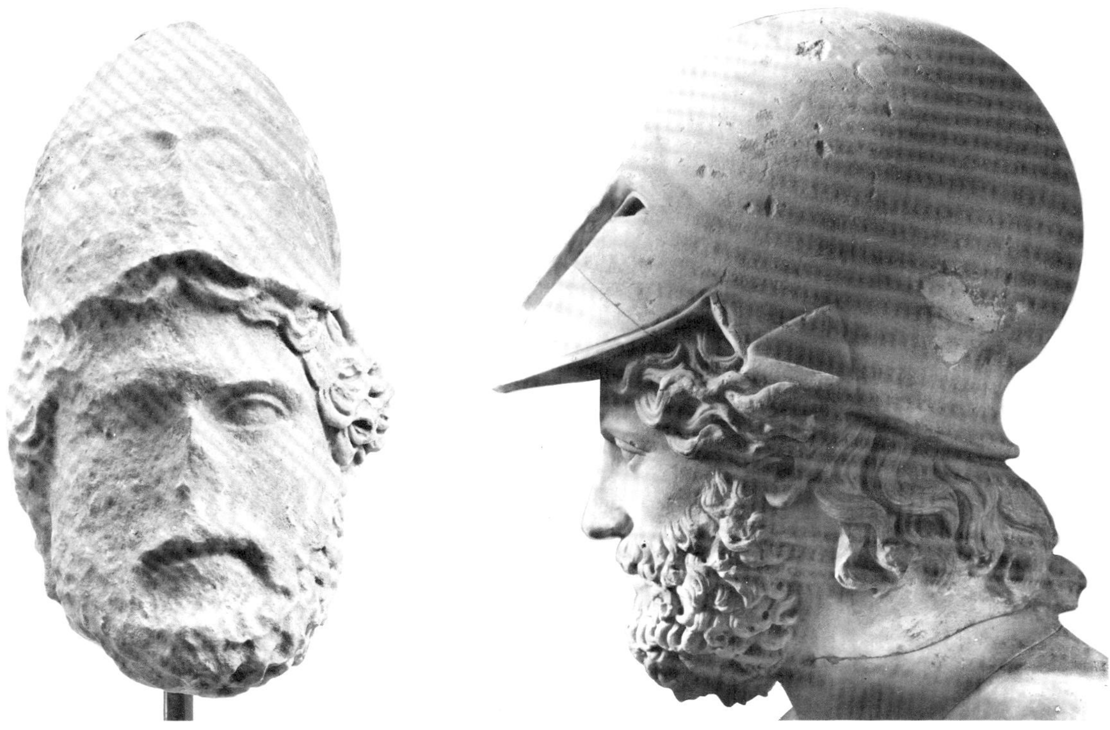

Figure 88. *Xanthippos. Roman marble head after a mid fifth century B.C. bronze original by Pheidias. Berlin, Pergamon Museum.*

1. **Xanthippos** This portrait is second chronologically in the series of surviving portraits of Athenian strategoi. The style corresponds to the middle of the fifth century B.C. His companion Anakreon (fig. 36) can be well compared to a figure on the shield of the Athena Parthenos, which confirms the attribution of both to Pheidias. There is still something suggesting an earlier date, perhaps a hint of expression that has not yet reached full classical serenity, remaining in the serious mood of early classicism. The abundant hair and beard, springing under the helmet, is also an earlier feature. We can perhaps reconstruct the group in imagination with the poet singing, his head thrown back, while his friend the general listens to the tune, somewhat in the manner of the group of *Athena and Marsyas* by Myron. Dedicating the two portraits on the Acropolis before the middle of the century, Perikles acclaimed not only his father's military successes but also how the family had traditionally been involved in the cultural life of Athens. For the identification see above pp. 14–16.

2

2

fig. 90

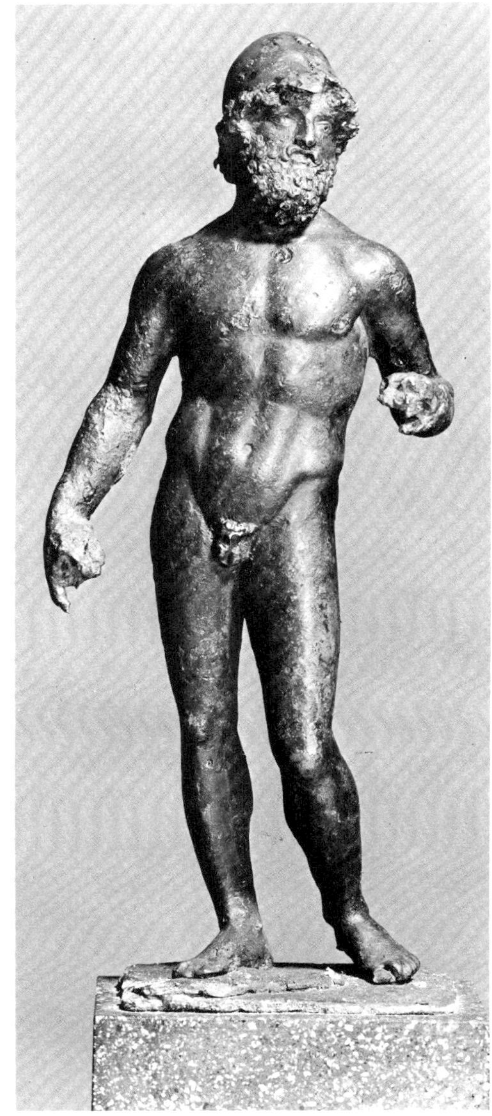

fig. 89

2. **Statuette of a strategos** The statuette reproduces with some alterations a larger statuette in the Wadsworth Atheneum, Hartford, (fig. 90) changing the gesture of both arms. In our replica the right hand holds a spear which was in the left hand in Hartford. The correspondence between the two confirms the truthfulness of the reduced bronze replicas for the reconstruction of the original. The body type follows the Polykleitan stance in a more subtle articulation, perhaps already from the beginning of the fourth century. The head type reproduced the so-called Pastoret strategos (fig. 89), known in several copies. The original is generally considered to reproduce the statue of Konon who escaped the battle of Aigospotamoi (405) and then with the help of Persian ships successfully battled Sparta, helping the restored democracy to recapture at least some part of Athenian power.

The rich hair and animated expression correspond well to the new style of portrait as inaugurated in the fifth century by Demetrios of Alopeke. The statuette and of course the life-size head replicas may well reproduce the monument that the thankful Athenian people erected in the Agora as the first image of an individual dedicated by the city since the monument to the Tyrant Slayers a century before—and the first public Athenian monument to a living man.

2. Konon (?)

Roman small bronze statuette with the head of the so-called Pastoret strategos of before 390 B.C. The presentation, including the silver inlays and frontality, corresponds well to the taste of Augustan classicism.

Figure 89. ***Roman marble head of an Athenian general after a very early fourth century B.C. bronze statue. Copenhagen, Ny Carlsberg Glyptotek.***

Figure 90. ***Roman bronze statuette reproducing the statue of an Athenian general from the beginning of the fourth century B.C. Hartford, Wadsworth Atheneum.***

3. Strategos

Roman marble after a bronze by Leochares from the third quarter of the fourth century B.C. Even from the head alone it is evident that the statue was in violent movement.

***3.* Strategos** In the view of archaeologists, the place of this portrait has wandered from the late fifth century (then called Alkibiades) to the end of the third century (recently attributed to the school of Phyromachos). Comparison with the helmeted strategos-like head of Leukippos, half-mythological founder of Metapontum, on the coins of this city (fig. 91), confirms the traditional dating early in the third quarter of the fourth century. The style, as shown especially by the best replica in the Metropolitan Museum, confirms not only the date but also that the portrait of Philip II (no. 4) must be by the same hand—perhaps Leochares. The proportions are identical; there is the same emphasis on the cheek bones, harmonizing with the arch of the eyebrows, and one receives in both cases the impression of a rather pale skin, something surprising in Greek sculpture but perhaps compatible with the appearance of ivory carving as practiced by Leochares. The preceding strategos, Xanthippos, is classically quiet; this head shows little more than personal features, but violent emotions inspire this general to action and his sculptor to art. Also, the mid-fifth century ideal of classical beauty is somewhat changed here from a pure, rather constructed appearance to a more anatomically casual rendering. The complete statue of this portrait may be preserved in two excellent small bronzes (Vienna and private collection (fig. 92)). The strategos was represented in violent movement, the nude is well comparable to the Belvedere Apollo—another point in favor of the atribution to Leochares.

fig. 92b

fig. 92a

fig. 92a

fig. 91

Figure 91. *Silver coin of Metapontum with the helmeted head of Leukippos, mythical founder of the city. Malibu, The J. Paul Getty Museum, presented by D. Rinne.*

Figure 92a. *Head of a large Roman bronze statuette with similar stance to no. 3, after an original from the third quarter of the fourth century B.C. Vienna, Kunsthistorisches Museum.*

Figure 92b. *Roman bronze statuette after the same original as no. 3 and fig. 91. Private collection.*

4. Philip What remains in this portrait of the real likeness of Alexander's father? Not even an allusion to the fact that he lost an eye. His indomitable nature is reduced to a slightly romantic image, but every distinctive feature has been smoothed in the frame of the Greek artistic tradition. There is no suggestion of the imperious personality of the man, including his half-barbarian background. Little is known about the art of Leochares, the Athenian sculptor who was a contemporary of Lysippos, but he is said to have been traditional in his approach. This Philip, together with some images of the youthful Alexander, may fit in his workshop.

It is worth notice that a bronze replica of the same face was found in the Villa dei Papiri. A twisted fillet was added by the Roman copyist, stemming from the Persian tradition adopted after Philip's death by Alexander and his successor kings. The head is part of a gallery including the youthful Alexander, Aristotle (Alexander's teacher), and possibly Diogenes (famous because of his witty encounter with Alexander).

4. Philip II

Roman copy after an original by Leochares. The violent nature of Alexander the Great's father is ennobled to the pattern of Greek classicism.

fig. 93

fig. 94

5

Figure 93. ***Philosopher. Roman marble head after the Greek original of no. 5. Rome, Palazzo dei Conservatori.***

Figure 94. ***Philosopher. Roman marble head reproducing the same original as no. 5 and fig. 93. Copenhagen, National Museum.***

5. Philosopher This and the following portrait were found together; the workmanship of the Roman copyist is identical, as is the general presentation. As stated above they were intended to be viewed together as a "gallery." They were in some ways pendants, and as both look like absent-minded professors, they must have been philosophers. The first is preserved in two other replicas, of which ours is by far the best (compare figs. 93 and 94). One would like to say he was the more famous of the two, but it may be purely a result of chance. He is the more good-natured of the two, with a gentle and indulgent smile. He also does not admit his age: very old, he is still shown with all his teeth, not as a result of the vanity of the man but a convention of the sculptor to conform to the trend of the time. Old age is "in" only from the late third century on, and the original of the portrait is not too far from Plato, i.e. around the middle of the fourth century. But age is revealed by the deeply sunken eyes with their dried-up eyelids. The close parallel with the portrait of Lysias and to some extent with Plato, together with the subtle psychology, play in favor of an attribution to Silanion.

5

5

5. Herm of a philosopher

Roman copy is an original from the early third quarter of the fourth century B.C. The well-advanced age of the sitter is denied in the best classical tradition.

6. Philosopher The comparison with the preceding philosopher does not hide his age. He is plainly toothless. The flesh of his face is dried and sunken. He has a prominent Adam's apple and tendons in his scrawny neck; even the collarbones and ribs in the bottom of the bust stand out. He is also much less good-hearted than his partner. Philosophizing must have turned him slightly bitter. He is kept out of his chronological order only because of his pairing with no. 5, as the style, physiognomy, and character can be better compared with the poet no. 43 of the first half of the second century B.C. and perhaps with Pseudo-Seneca (fig. 86). No name can be suggested and no exact replicas are known.

6. Herm of a philosopher

Roman copy after an original from the first half of the second century B.C. The bitter character of the sitter is rendered without hesitation as is his old age.

7

7. Thucydides

Roman copy after an original from the third quarter of the fourth century B.C. The portrait is hardly recognizeable because of the secondary modification.

Figure 95. *Thucydides. Roman marble head after a Greek bronze original from the third quarter of the fourth century B.C. Budapest, Museum of Fine Arts.*

7

7

7

fig. 95

7

7. Thucydides 1 Who would believe that this is Thucydides? Once you cover the lower part of the face, however, the identification in comparison with well-preserved other replicas becomes self-evident (see fig. 95). As in other cases we are too used to looking at works of art as part of museum inventories, where they remain well protected and immutable unless something happens. But a good head portrait in Roman times would not be destroyed or disposed of even after an accident: it would simply be recut to continue in service under another name.

The original quality was good: an image of the strong and severe personality of the great historian as conceived less than a century after his death, presenting the same concision as his own work. Objectivity and distance by their very nature create a feeling of stronger personality than any other of the ancient classics. The image must have been created in the third quarter of the fourth century in remembrance of the past grandeur of Athens. From then on, Athens would no longer be important because of its living history but because of its dead.

fig. 96

8

8. Thucydides

Roman marble after a bronze original of the later third century B.C. This is the second, more animated, representation of the great historian.

Figure 96. *Thucydides. Roman marble head after a Greek original from the third century B.C. Corfu, Museum.*

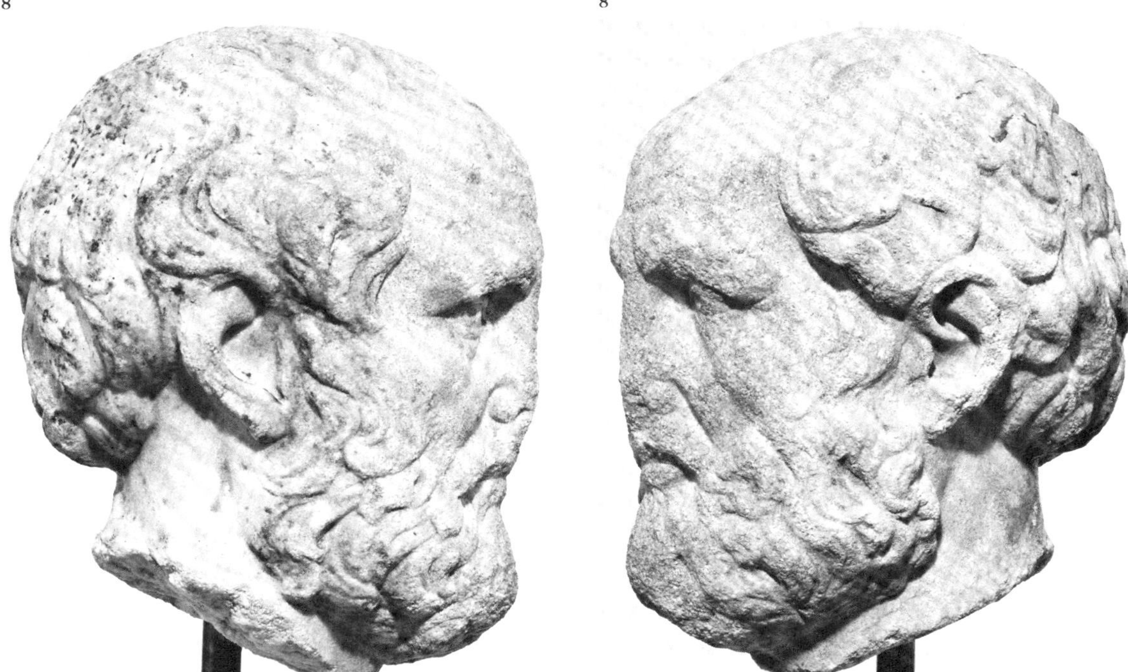

8 8

***8.* Thucydides (Corfu type)** This is not the proper place for the style of this head. The original points to the third century at least. It is here because of its possible identity. It is a close variant of the head in Corfu (fig. 96) which is called Thucydides by some, although the identification is denied by others. The confrontation of the canonical Thucydides from the fourth century makes it difficult. Even the division of the beard is different; the man looks more anxious, considerably older, shorter, and much more "real" than the inscribed type of Thucydides. This is approximately how the Athenians of about 280 B.C., when decreeing a public statue of Demosthenes, may well have seen the incorruptible master historian describing the century of their glory: with equal attention to their fortunes and their shortcomings, the latter with anxiety in their hearts, as this portrait shows well. The man is so real that one hardly accepts it as a retrospective creation.

***9.* Plato** The Greek workmanship, from the pre-Roman period, produces some hesitation over the identification of this head. But already in the first publication notice it was said, "the portrait of Plato is its nearest kin." Indeed, it is Plato. The variations in details are due to the reduced scale and to the fact that exact mechanically-achieved copies are scarce until the time of Augustus and frequent only from the time of Hadrian on. However, this is perhaps the most enjoyable Plato of some twenty surviving replicas. What is lacking in precision of rendering Silanion's original is gained in liveliness and rather pleasant character of the greatest poet among Greek philosophers. Usually in the most correct copies Silanion's Plato appears like a morose professor with spoiled digestion. Here we have an image of the author who wrote *Symposion*, suffered through his emotive involvements, and dreamed like hardly any other Greek.

9. Plato

Late Hellenistic version after the seated statue by Silanion, dedicated in the Athenian Academy before the middle of the fourth century B.C. In spite of the small scale, the freshness of the still Greek carving ranks the piece among the best likenesses of the great philosopher.

10 10 10

***10.* Plato** This too is a Plato. The identification, after some initial hesitation, is beyond doubt. The orientation corresponds well to the original seated statue by Silanion, but it is hard to recognize the man. Not only are the locks of hair utterly different but also the modeling of the anatomical structure of the face is flattened and minimized to such a degree that the sitter appears falsely rejuvenated. It is no longer a triumph of the spirit over the flesh because the flesh is turning to inarticulate, dead stone. This is how the attempt to resuscitate Platonism that started in the beginning of the third century A.D. saw its supposed father-founder: pure spirit with the enormous eyes turned toward heaven, completely detached from any reality. There are other neo-Platonic visions of Plato. Ours at least provides the most gentle appearance for the prevailing age of spirituality.

11

11

11. **Double herm: Plato and Aristotle** The sculpture was carved as a purely decorative piece; the cavities on the sides were intended to insert the plain slabs of a fence. Thus the portraits were meant only as reminders or suggestions of the two philosophers. This was much more important than the precision of the copy and the low artistic quality. The association of Plato, the great master, and Aristotle, his best if not completely faithful pupil, is self explanatory. Plato is much easier to recognize with his dyspeptic grimace, even if the number and shape of the hair locks is far from the canonical type. Aristotle, on the other hand, passed through a completely cosmetic surgery of his appearance. While the standard replicas reproduce correctly the heroic attempt to disguise the progressive baldness of the philosopher, here the lack of hair above the forehead is stated with an exaggerated frankness. Even the vault of the skull turns from magnitude to caricature. The spontaneous early third century A.D. approach of the provincial sculptor brings forward more naivete than real competence, not only in rendering the spirit of the portrait but also even in the simple craftsmanship. One would like to explain this from the Egyptian tradition—but there is none.

10. Plato

Late Roman marble after Silanion's original. The rejuvenated face has lost both bones and musculature in a Neoplatonic, purely spiritual, interpretation of Plato.

11. Double herm: Plato and Aristotle

Early third century A.D. decorative work used as the crown of a fence post, expressing the intellectual preoccupation of a rich provincial.

12

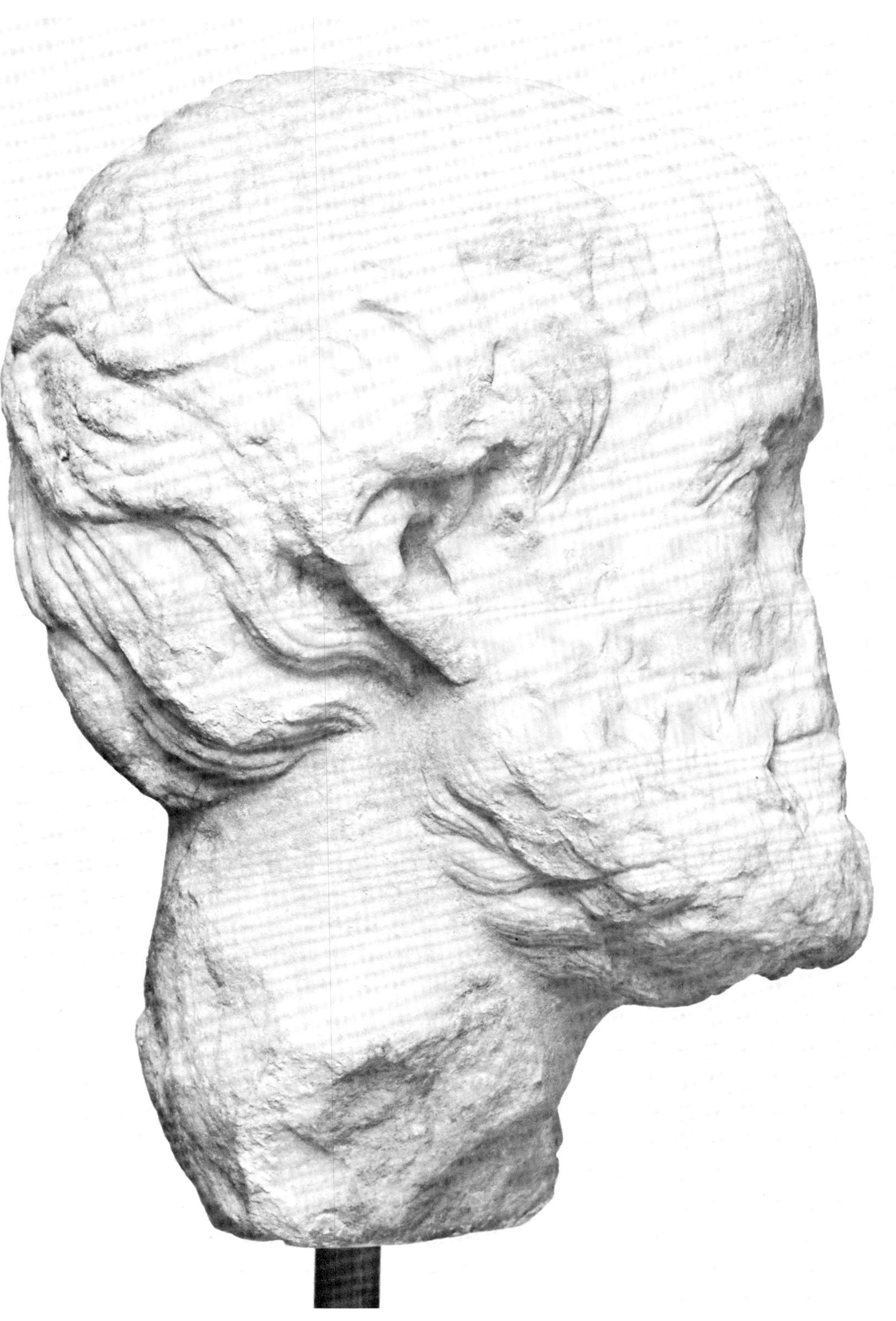

12. Aristotle

Roman marble copy of a bronze original by Lysippos from about 330 B.C. This was the first instance when Greek art came close to our modern conception of portraiture.

12

11

13

***12.* Aristotle** The portrait, preserved in many replicas, was very popular in Roman times. The bronze original has rightly been connected with Lysippos—a Roman herm on the Acropolis, probably only a shadowy memory of the original, is inscribed as a dedication of Alexander to his divine teacher. Our replica is conscientious and correct, but the poor preservation and rather impressionistic treatment of the surface fail to provide much of an idea about the strength of the piece. There is, however, still not only the deep intellect and utterly individual appearance but also some hint that the man cared for his appearance, including a heroic attempt to conceal his baldness. Some archaeologists would prefer to place the original in the early third century, but the close relationship with the Euripides type Farnese (no. 15) prevents it. Another confirmation of the earlier date is the fact that the head is "quoted" as an accepted type on at least one Attic grave stele from the 20s of the fourth century. It must further have made a permanent impression in the world of Athenian portraiture. At least two extant images from the first half of the third century follow its general patterns (one of them our no. 39).

13

14 14

13. Aristotle

A simplified image in local stone evidencing the respect of a remote province for a great classic.

***13.* Aristotle** This is a free reproduction of the standard portrait type. The provincial sculptor simplified the rich modeling, the subtle indication of psychology, and the "gentle" effort to mask the baldness with a thin but elegant fringe of hair. But the basic elements of the portrait are retained sufficiently to recognize the man and even his philosophical "character" is maintained. The merit of the piece is twofold, showing the approach of a provincial workmanship and demonstrating also the universal reputation of a great man. Finally there is the fact that the head was part of a gallery from which now at least one other piece is known to survive—the following one—but which must have included other, possibly many other, images of Greek classics. Even the remote and mostly barbarian Haurân benedited from the radiation of Greek culture under the *pax Romana*.

***14.* Thespis (?)** The workmanship is identical with the preceding head of Aristotle (no. 13): compare especially the linear rendering of the eyelids and the soft but determined modeling of the cheekbones. The two heads from the same material reached the museum by different routes but could be traced to the same source. We would like to see their origin in a large architectonic complex exhibiting the simplified likenesses of great men in the past, something in the spirit of many American public buildings in the nineteenth century.

The identification of the man is purely hypothetical. It is proposed because the face is not a real portrait; it is more a genre image, the expressive mimics and funnel-like lips together with the overshadowed eyes remind one of a theatrical mask. Thus it is much more a reconstructed fantasy portrait than a direct image of a well-individualized person. The existence of a statue commemorating the sixth century B.C. founder of Attic tragedy is evidenced by an inscribed base of Roman date found in the theater of Dionysos in Athens. And what could be more convincing than association of Thespis, founder of the tragedy, with Aristotle, its best theoretician. While the original of Aristotle goes back to Lysippos, the original of Thespis reveals the baroque qualities of early second century B.C. art, a good comparison being provided by the heads of the great Altar from Pergamon.

14. Thespis (?)

Provincial copy of an imaginary representation created to pair the founder of tragedy with its eminent theoretician—Aristotle (no. 13).

15 15

***15.* Euripides** At first glance our replica seems considerably different from the established type. The locks of hair and details are all there, but the general impression seems to lack the power of, say, the Farnese copy in Naples (fig. 59) where one can feel the advanced age, including the toothless gums and the general melancholy in the character of a poet. This is because the craftsmanship is authentically Greek. Like some other copies (especially the one in Budapest) it must have been carved in the eastern part of the Roman world, possibly even in Greece itself. Thus the quality of modeling is stronger than the subtle nuances of catching the individual characteristics. The straight position of the neck does not correspond to the seated statue of the Lysippic Euripides.

15. Euripides

Second to first century A.D. marble replica of Greek workmanship after a bronze seated statue by Lysippos from the 30s of the fourth century B.C. The artistic qualities of the marble are higher than its faithfulness to the original.

16

16. Herm of Solon (?)

Roman marble after a bronze connected with Lysippos from the late fourth century B.C. It must represent one of the Seven Wise Men, but the identification of this imaginary portrait is not certain.

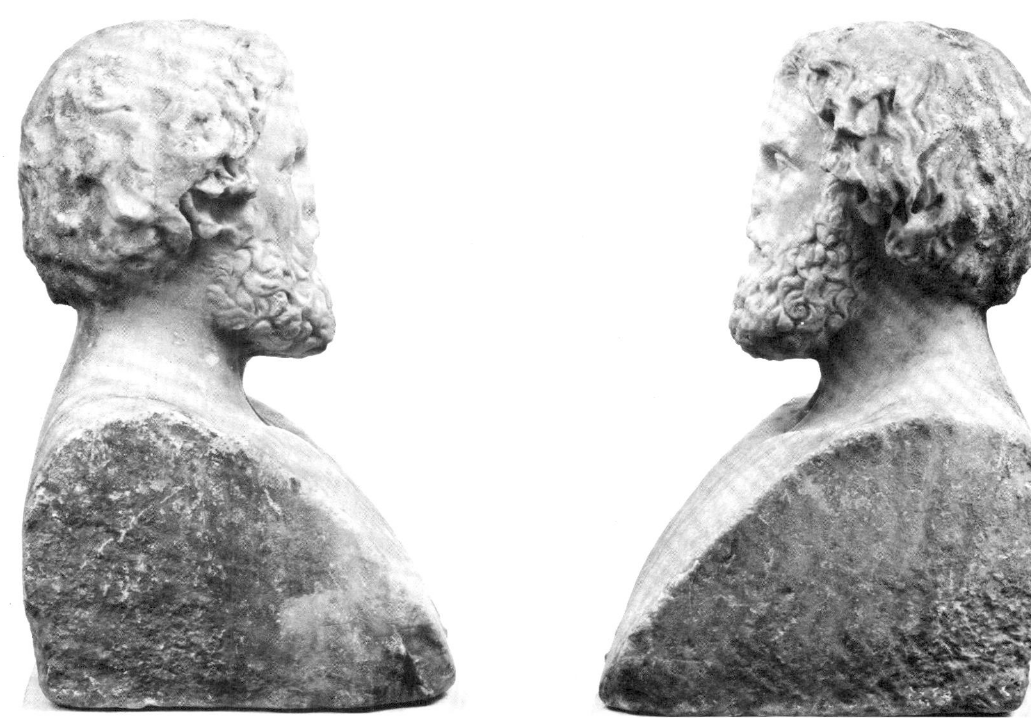
16 16

16. **Herm of Solon (?)** This is manifestly a reconstructed portrait. There is nothing too evident in the features to suggest a real personality, and this fits well with other preserved *Fantasienbildnisse* of the Seven Wise Men. Ours has the largest number of replicas. This means it must have been the most popular, the best known of the Seven. Thus two candidates are possible: Solon, the real father of the Athenian city-state, or Thales, who won the contest of wisdom among the Seven themselves. The beard points rather to Solon, as the painted representation of Thales is Ostia is beardless; but nothing is completely sure. The replica and its preservation are excellent. The style is indisputably Lysippic.

17

17

17

17. Periander

Roman marble after the bronze by Lysippos from the late fourth century B.C. Modern intervention disfigured the well-known portrait type.

***17.* Periander** The modern alterations opened doubts about this piece or, at least, about its exact chronological classification. Repeated examination of the modern changes rescued the marble head as a late first century A.D. copy of a late fourth century original close to the well-established iconography of Periander, one of the Seven Wise Men and by his profession tyrant of Corinth in the very early sixth century B.C. One of the best if not most complete copies was seen to be compatible with the portrait of Aristotle, establishing the same sculptor—Lysippos—for the original. It is hard to see from our specimen, where even the identification is not clear at once, but the general conception of a rather small head is clearly Lysippic. The closest companion is Solon (no. 16). In all other images of the Seven Wise Men, Lysippos varied a kind of a *characteris* in the way of Aristotle's immediate follower Theophrastos. They are all clearly wise, proto-philosophers, but each is different from the others in general mood rather than in personal features. Against the charismatic wisdom of Solon, Periander appears not only younger but also as a restrained man of action.

18

18

18

18. Herm of Aischines

Roman marble after the Greek bronze from the late 30s of the fourth century B.C. The ancient inscription gives the piece the false identity of Periander.

18. **Aischines** Aischines, the leader of the pro-Macedonian faction in Athens, went into voluntary exile after he lost his action in court against Demosthenes. He settled on Rhodes and may have there had his statue executed during his lifetime. Contrary to opinions that would put the original only in the third century B.C., there is a clear comparison with the Lycourgan Sophokles (fig. 56) and contemporary Panatheniac prize amphoras, surely still from the 30s of the fourth century. But the workmanship of the bronze original seems rather to be Attic, including the proportions, the treatment of the drapery preserved in the complete statue replica, and the characteristics. But there could have been a traveling Attic sculptor in Rhodes. The result is a polished man with good manners and countenance opposed to the ebullience of Demosthenes (at least following the portrait), but Demosthenes' image (no. 40) dates at least half a century later. The broken herm in the Getty Museum must have been much better than one could guess from its present state. The inscription giving the name of Periander is ancient, eloquent evidence for misidentification.

19

20

20

19

fig. 97

fig. 98

19 and 20. **Alexander and Hephaistion** The prototype of Alexander goes back to the youthful portrait, possibly created by Leochares, erected probably in Athens during Alexander's short visit there in 338 (see fig. 60). Among the most easily perceived changes is the hair, executed with an abundance greater than in the latest versions of portraits from Alexander's lifetime. A kind of eternal youth, like a memento from the Elysian Fields, calms the usual brilliance of the conquering hero.

Hephaistion is carved as a pendant to his friend and master. More conservative, he shows less brio and less will than his friend.

As portraits the two heads are surely not strongly individualized, but as works of art they belong in spite of later, though still ancient, recutting among the best works of ancient art in the Getty Museum. United in their posthumous glory as they were in tender friendship, Alexander and Hephaistion presided over a great commemorative monument of some other Greek, enhancing his immortality. In the same function they appear on the reliefs decorating the sarcophagus of a rather insignificant king of Sidon in Phoenicia (the so-called Alexander Sarcophagus).

19. Alexander

Greek marble from ca. 320 B.C. Posthumous rejuvenated image of the great conqueror.

20. Hephaistion

Greek marble from ca. 320 B.C. Conventional portrait of Alexander's best friend.

Figure 97. *Head of a flute player. Marble head from the same group as Alexander, Hephaistion, and the princess. Late fourth century B.C. Malibu, The J. Paul Getty Museum.*

Figure 98. *Princess with elaborate hairstyle. Marble head from the same group as Alexander, Hephaistion, and the flute player. Late fourth century B.C. Malibu, The J. Paul Getty Museum.*

21

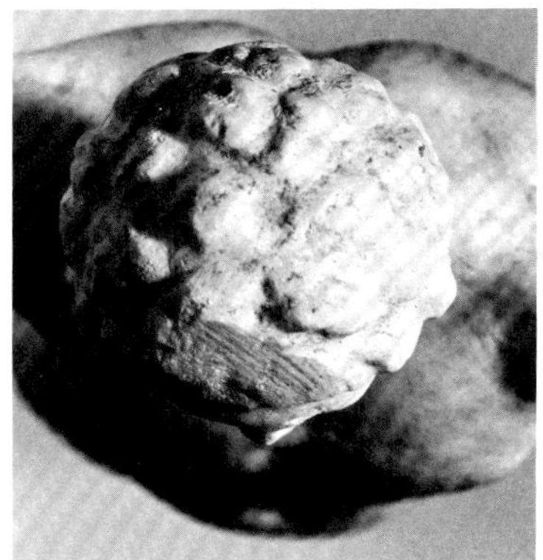

21

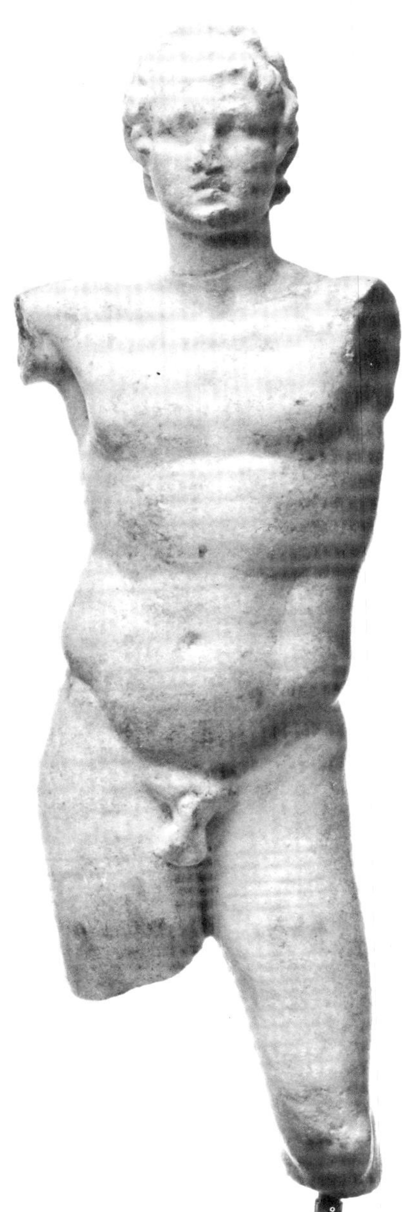

24 bis

21. Alexander

Marble Hellenistic version of the famous Lysippan bronze statue of Alexander with the Lance from the 20s of the fourth century B.C.

24 bis. Alexander as Sarapis

A later image of the great ruler assimilated to the Ptolemaic divinity.

***21.* Statuette of Alexander the Great** The statuette, carved with freshness and elegance, seems to be a reproduction of Lysippos' Alexander with the Lance with some small variations. The overall appearance is rather soft although strongly articulated. The effect is more elegant than powerful. A competent sculptor of the second century B.C. modified the general conception into already neoclassical image. Also Lysippos' Alexander, even in small scale replicas, is distinctly developed in space. Our piece is markedly frontal. The pose of holding the lance was originally full of action but here turns to a theatrical presentation. The modeling also gains a softer quality, typical for an experienced marble carver, unifying the great surfaces of the bronze original. The artistic quality is outstanding.

22

23

24

***22.* Alexander** Already during his lifetime Alexander was, according to his own wishes, elevated to the level of the gods. The apotheosis took on new dimensions after his death. Among many divine surnames he assumed—Hermes, Dioskouros, Herakles—one was particularly favored, Alexander-Helios, not only because the artistic parallels between the types created for Alexander and for the god but also for the background idea of Sol, master of the cosmos, with Alexander as the prototype of a ruler of all the earth. Images of this type multiplied during the Roman Empire, freely reproducing types from the Hellenistic period. Our head is just such a work. To produce the effect of a solar divinity, Alexander was adorned with metal spikes fixed in the holes drilled in his rich locks of hair. Because of its conservation, the head has little more than statistical value.

***23.* Small head of Alexander** The little head of Alexander may once have been a pleasant Alexandrian product. Its preservation must have been disastrous, while an incompetent modern hand tried to return it to some human shape. Already during this repair process the head must have looked worse and worse, but the good intentions of the modern vandal could not stop halfway. There is no doubt about the authenticity of the piece, but in its current state it is just another bit of evidence for Alexander's popularity throughout antiquity in the city he founded and in which he was buried.

***24.* Bronze statuette of a Hellenistic ruler, probably Alexander** Given the small dimensions, the identification remains only hypothetical. The *anastole* and proportions of the face remind one strongly of Alexander the Great. Statuettes of this low quality must have been produced in Roman times in mass quantities, corresponding to the widespread admiration for the hero who remained the prototype of Roman emperors from Caesar (with whom he is compared by Plutarch) through Caracalla (who aped him) until Constantine.

***24 bis.* Alexander-Sarapis** With sandals and chlamys—short mantle—Alexander stands holding a palm branch in his left hand. Another object, held in the right hand, is broken off and undistinguishable. The cylindrical modius on his head is the attribute of the god Serapis, widely supported by the Ptolemies as the divine associate of their rule. The modius is here associated with another crown, partially broken off. The luxuriant hair frames the face which maintains the basic features of Alexander, slightly modified by the Hellenistic style.

22. Alexander as Helios

Poorly presented indifferent marble of Roman times.

23. Alexander

Small Hellenistic head annihilated by modern intervention.

24. Alexander (?)

Bronze Roman statuette.

25

25. The Getty Bronze

Bronze statue of ca. 320–310 B.C. Hellenistic prince from a family of Alexander's successors as a victor in the Olympic Games by Lysippos.

25

25

26

26

26

***25/26.* The Getty Bronze and a marble herm representing the same sitter** The masterpiece presents many facets to the viewer: eternal youth, the exaltation of victory. The only aspect that interests us here, however, is how far he represents an individual. The two profiles, especially the left one, show a face deviating from Greek canons of ideal beauty, personalized even more than the standard images of Alexander the Great. One could say that the boy is very conscious of his glorious achievement, that he is also very strong willed, and there is little if any softness in him. The sharp, pointed nose and the eyes slightly less open than usual, together with the willfully compressed lips, are the most striking personal features. Thus, the degree of individuality of perception of a concrete person is clearly marked. But it hardly leaves the frame of two more general themes, winning and belonging to the aristocracy of Greece; and his expectations correspond to his noble origins.

It seems likely that the same man appears twenty years older in another sculpture, illuminating many problems of Greek portraiture. It is a poor Roman replica in the form of a herm. The man is now the ruler; he wears a simple diadem, rather than an olive crown of victory at Olympia. Another replica, also a herm, was found at Ephesos, and the reflections of the same face can be traced in other marbles. At first glance the man does not age, but closer inspection shows that he did. There is much less character, but the flesh is heavier. He was the young prince, self-confident and at the moment of victory. Now we look at the official image and see the personal appearance and psychology limited. The parallel with Alexander, so personal in the Getty Bronze, is reduced to a general indication of a ruler who claims the same roots and legitimacy. The man disappears, diluted in his divine function.

The comparison defines negatively how much the Getty Bronze is a portrait. In positive terms, the sculpture achieves a balance between the general type and the individual: the bronze is still ideal and has divine, incomparable beauty, giving the overwhelming impression of the moment of victory; he is also boyish and unrestrainable: in short, a young eagle.

The attribution of the Bronze to Lysippos is confirmed by comparison with the head of the Apoxyomenos and with the face of the Azara Alexander (fig. 64). There is an interesting comparison between the statue and a Roman fresco with two figures, including a young athletic victor crowning himself with olive and holding a palm branch. It is interpreted as reflecting a creation by Eupompos, a Sicyonian painter who is said to have influenced the young Lysippos. The identification of the person represented in the Getty Bronze needs further research.

26. Herm of a Hellenistic Ruler

Roman marble after a bronze from the early third century B.C. The sitter may be the same person as represented in the Getty Bronze, only twenty-thirty years older: no more the victorious athlete but a consecrated, impersonal ruler.

fig. 99

27

Figure 99. *Demetrios Poliorketes. Small quartzite head from the very early third century B.C. Geneva, Museum of Art and History.*

fig. 99

27

27

***27.* Head of a youth** This attractive original Greek sculpture is a borderline portrait. The face is obviously individualized but not enough to give the impression of a well-defined personality. However, the art is subtle and fine, both in modeling and in characterization. The originally added bronze fillet was suitable for a ruler, but the piece carved in Athens in the third century seems *at first* to be a bit out of context. A full-size head of a ruler would be a conventional expression of a city's adulation of a benefactor or a menace, but this is clearly a small, private piece. The marble head, from one or two generations after the heroic age of the Getty Bronze, is of completely different stuff. The sitter may have had a weight problem.

His identification is established by comparison with a small quarzite head recently acquired by the Musée d'Art et d'Histoire in Geneva (fig. 99). Both countenances seem to be the same, but the Geneva head also bears a key to its identify: two small bull's horns above the forehead are the attributes of Demetrios Poliorketes, and our head thus perpetuates a memorial to the liberator of Athens in 310. The coins of Demetrios confirm the identification. Our head dates somewhat later, in the third century, perhaps before Demetrios's inglorious final years. The official portrait of the last real heir of Alexander's dreams of empire was created by a follower of Lysippos, and it may survive in some Roman copies. Our small head is an independent Attic creation of outstanding quality.

27. Demetrios Poliorketes

Small Attic original work of the second quarter of the third century B.C. (?). This little head is an indisputable masterpiece, but it does not render well the legendary charisma of this ruler.

28

28

28. Ptolemy II

Mid third century B.C. After the death of the king, an elephant-head helmet was added to the portrait to make it more impressive.

29

30

31

32

28. **Ptolemy II** The colossal size for rulers' monuments started with Alexander the Great. This is a good example but the head is not particularly attractive; the end of our second millenium has seen too many colossal images of strong rulers. The poor preservation does not improve the appraisal but the craftsmanship was originally excellent. The rich modeling of the surely-not-lean flesh presents West Asian Hellenistic art at its best.

The person responsible for the second presentation tried his best: the elephant-head helmet, nailed over the cut-down hair must have been even more grandiose and garish than the depiction of the man himself, but one has to follow with some sympathy the desperate attempt to raise the prestige of the fat ruler after his death. The piece clearly belongs to a period when "big" and "great" became synonymous.

29–30–31. **Small heads of Ptolemy III and IV** The two small and one very small head clearly belong to Ptolemaic iconography, and they dramatize the iconographic problems associated with the portraits of that family: the difficulty of distinguishing among the mass products expressing the loyalty the inhabitants of Alexandria nourished for their changing sovereigns. The style shows minimal evolution and the individual features are sometimes very hard to make out, especially for our smallest head. Were they clear for the contemporary viewers? Or was their enthusiasm for their kings, who were in fact changing, chased, and returning to the throne, above such trifles as identification? The most important thing was the show. Thus while there is hesitation over the names of the two larger heads, the third piece—the worst preserved although perhaps the most pleasant originally—is set apart by its more clearly sculptural definition and better probability for the designation of the ruler.

32. **Head of a late Ptolemy as pharaoh** The undetermined Ptolemy is represented with a pharaoh's headdress, including the uraeus. A grid is incised on the back: the piece served as a sculptor's model and these indications served for transferring the measurements to the actual sculpture during the carving process. This was a traditional way of carving, and the whole schema is also Egyptian, but the modeling of the cheeks and lips clearly betrays Greek influence. The precise identification as one of the latest Ptolemies is yet to be ascertained.

29. Ptolemy III

Conventional small head from the late third century B.C.

30. Ptolemy IV (?)

Conventional portrait from the end of the third century B.C.

31. Ptolemy IV

Ruined small head from the early second century B.C.

32. Head of a late Ptolemy as pharaoh

A sculptor's model from the first century B.C. (?). The Egyptian schema constitutes the frame while details of the anatomy betray the Greek tradition.

33. Seleucid ruler

Roman marble copy from the first half of the second century B.C. The craftsmanship is rather schematic; the original was a powerful creation of the Hellenistic Baroque.

33 33

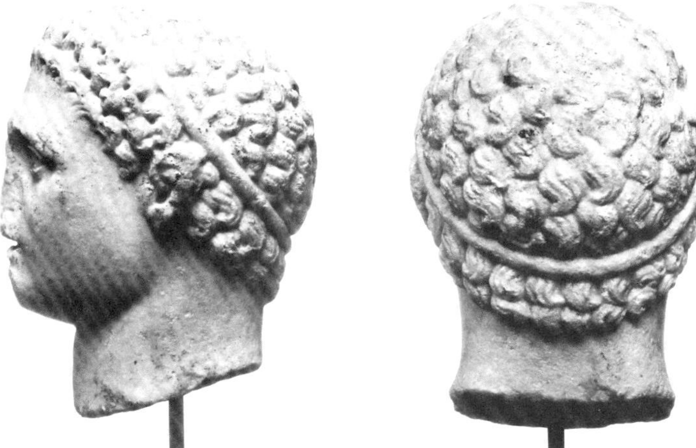

fig. 100

33. **Head of a Hellenistic ruler** The copy was intended for a herm, as seen from the flat rendering of the nape. The Roman craftsman simplified the appearance, emphasizing at the same time the baroque expression. Several coin portraits of different Hellenistic rulers may be compared with no definite decision possible on the identification, but the closest analogy is the head of a bronze statuette in Kansas City (fig. 100) called Seleukus IV Philopator of Syria; our piece must indeed be the same person even if the identification is not secure. The rather realistic rendering of the actual likeness corresponds well to the images of the rulers of the later Hellenistic period: they are god-chosen and and can therefore afford to look ugly.

Figure 100. ***Head of a Roman bronze statue representing perhaps Seleukos IV Philopator (ca. 218–175 B.C.). Kansas City, Nelson-Atkins Museum.***

34. Inscribed small bronze bust of Menander

Reduced Roman copy after the original statue from ca. 290 B.C. by the sons of Praxiteles. This small monument settled the much disputed identity of the sitter.

34

34 Inscription

MENANΔPOC

35

36

***34.* Menander 1** The small bronze bust has, of course, the merit of having settled some eighty years of discussion about the identity of the man surviving in about fifty copies. The partisans of Vergil were a minority; but now they have to give up unless their stubbornness helps them to maintain an absurdity. Besides this, the craftsmanship is of excellent quality, competent if not superior to the standard of the small bronze bust found in the Villa dei Papiri. The precise modeling may correspond to the end of the first century B.C./ early first century A.D.

35. Herm of Menander

Correct but cold Roman copy of the famous portrait.

36. Menander

The excellent replica, with rich modeling and expressive details, was completely ruined by modern recutting.

35

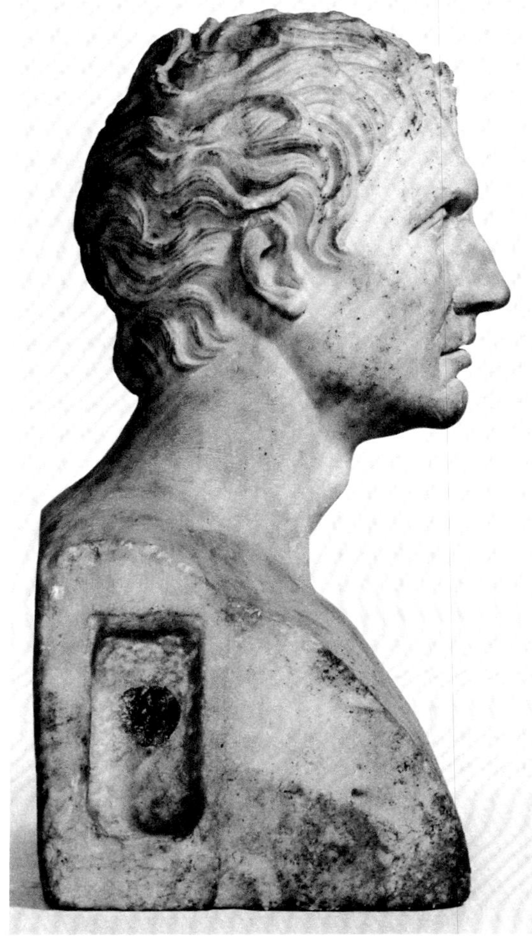

34

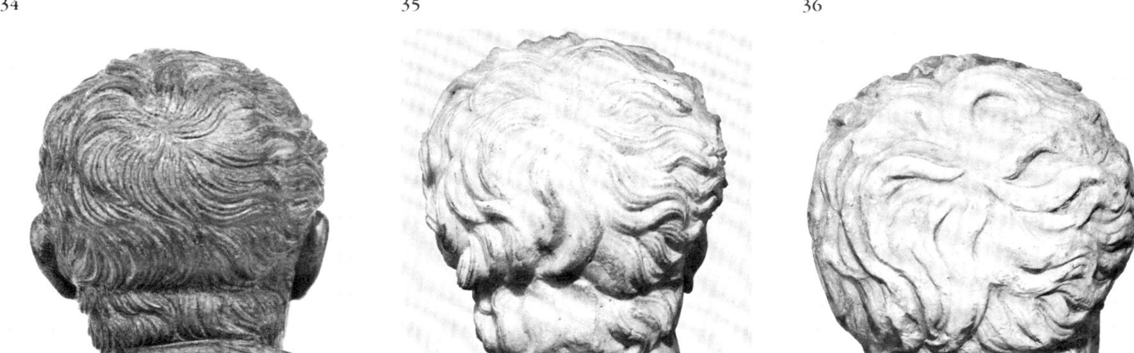

34 35 36

35–36. **Menander 2 and 3** Two marble replicas offer excellent possibilities for comparison and give at least some idea of how an original can be traced through Roman copies. The first has a pleasant appearance and is fairly well preserved. Except for the nose, everything survives and agrees with the majority of the other replicas. The resulting image is rather classicistic.

The other head is completely ruined. Only the hair gives prima facie evidence of how excellent the craftsmanship originally was. The subtlety of its modeling and of the sophisticated pattern preserved by the strands of hair provide a strong argument that this is how the original must have been done. Little remains intact from the face but the eyeballs, deeply set in the cavities and covered with parchment-like eyelids, ravaged by wrinkles and with tired bags under the eyes. Suddenly the work fits much better into the third century. There are more personal characteristics, more portraiture in Menander's face than the common image that is suggested by most of the replicas. From this we can return to the small bronze bust (no. 34). The slightly dry but rich description of the features translates more of the original than one admits at first glance.

The original must have been set up immediately after 291, the year of Menander's death. It was a seated statue created by Kephistodotos the Younger and Timarchos, sons of the great Praxiteles. We are told that Menander, the highly polished author, was before everything else an accomplished gentleman, a man of the world. The portrait depicts indeed a complex personality. The distinguished appearance, with the elegant hair fashion framing the face, does not hide a deep soul, still perhaps more tormented than it may seem at first glance. His philosophical background—a student of Aristotle's school under Theophrastos—may have fortified his cosmopolitanism; though while closely bound with his city, he avoided any involvement in the turmoil and vicissitudes of Athens in its decline during his lifetime.

37

37. Epicurus

Roman marble after the original statue from the second quarter of the third century B.C. This heart-breaking ruin was perhaps the best surviving replica of the image of the famous philosopher.

39

39

38

38

38

***37–38.* Epicurus** The seated statue of Epicurus was erected in his Garden after 271/270. As his philosophy was very popular with the Romans, replicas are abundant. Pliny states in the second quarter of the first century A.D. that "everybody has an image of Epicurus in his bedroom, and many carry it with them on their travels."

The larger of our replicas must have been superb. Viewing it in silhouette, we can still perceive something of the fire that animated the marble. Nothing of the cheap hedonism that is conventionally associated with the school, but the apotheosis of the spirit triumphing over the debility of the human condition as it was aptly put by his great Roman follower Lucretius:

> Thou, who out of deep darkness didst first avail to raise a torch so clear, shedding light upon the true joys of life, 'tis thee I follow, thou glory of the Greek race. . . . Thou are our father, the discoverer of truth. . . . He then who has subdued all these and driven them from the mind by speech, not arms, shall this man not rightly be found worthy to rank among the gods? (*De rerum natura*, III, 1–3, 9, V, 49–51)

The miniature head must have been broken off a statuette. It is slightly more summary than the lifesize one, but the workmanship is very precise. The powerful image was above the ability of the craftsman, but he did his best to preserve the general likeness and the quality of the modeling. Together with the portraits of two fellow Epicureans, Menandros, and some other images, the statue of Epicurus belongs to the rather classicizing trend of early Hellenistic portraiture.

***39.* Philosopher** The man must have been a philosopher. He has some of the Epicurean mildness, as best represented in the portrait type of Hemachos; but his hair style, beard, and physical type are clearly inspired by the portrait of Aristotle. The sitter may have been a Peripatetic philosopher.

The resemblance could also mean that the likeness of Aristotle as preserved by Lysippos became a kind of philosopher par excellence, a prototype for commemorating other professionals of thought. But while Aristotle is Lysippic, this head clearly claims the Attic tradition.

38. Small head of Epicurus

Broken from a statuette which may have stood on the desk of a Roman Epicurean.

39. Philosopher

Roman marble after a mid-third century B.C. Attic portrait. The original was psychologically very expressive.

40 40 40

***40.* Demosthenes** Around 280 B.C., in an act of repentant nostalgia, the Athenians dedicated a portrait statue of the great patriot, leader of their heroic and last fight for freedom. Represented as an orator, Demosthenes was recreated by Polyeuktos, a sculptor otherwise unknown. This likeness shows the inevitable progress of Hellenistic portraiture towards more concrete, more "real" depiction of individuals. Traditionally the serious appearance of the man and his deep involvement are played as "meaningful" for a "real" image. But there is another rather anatomical feature that is captured here and which must have been true to Demosthenes' physiognomy. We know that he had a speech impediment that he overcame with painful, constant practice, and indeed, seen from the side, Demosthenes' head reveals a receding lower jaw, a so-called bird profile. No other ancient head shows it, and it even escapes the modern viewer. The monument is consecrated to the intrepid, self-sacrificing democratic statesman who overcame a physical defect in the most Greek way.

***41.* Phokion** The identification of this portrait was already argued in the introduction (p. 36). It is the only strategos who comes close in style and characteristics to Phokion's contemporary Demosthenes; the original may also have been by Polyeuktos. The only other replica is more complete but retouched in modern times and was never too good. He is the most individual of all the strategoi portraits. Compared with Demosthenes, the expression of individuality is equally complex but shown with more restraint. So we gain the image of how the Athenians saw their most reliable and constant patriot, a general who disliked war, who was an aristocrat and did not hesitate after the disaster at Chaironeia to form a national unity with his political adversary Demosthenes, in short a true patriot *patriai tempore iniquo*. Not unlike Demosthenes' monument, the statue of Phokion expressed repentant reappraisal of a man condemned by the city to drink hemlock.

41

fig. 101

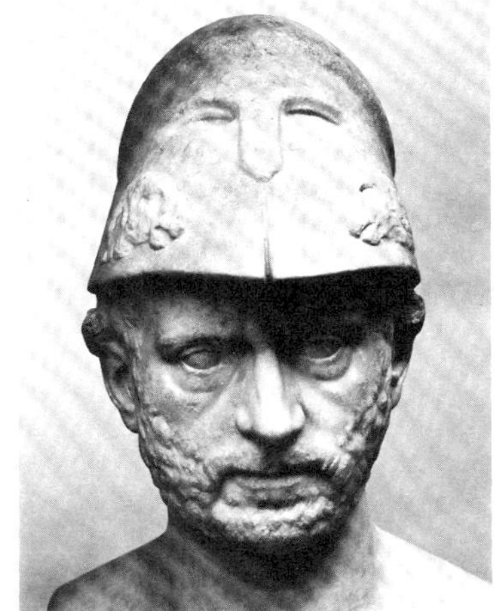

fig. 101

41

40. Demosthenes

Roman marble replica after the bronze statue erected ca. 280 B.C. in the Athenian marketplace. Our piece gives just the exterior features of the original masterpiece.

41. Phokion

Roman marble after a bronze statue from ca 280 B.C. The replica is of outstanding quality.

Figure 101. *Roman marble head (with some restorations and retouching) after an Attic original from the early third century B.C. East Berlin, Pergamon Museum.*

fig. 102

42

42. Poet

A contemporary of Demosthenes, the portrait is still rather classical—not revealing the sitter's great age—in spite of the strong characteristics. Carved in the later first century A.D. as a Roman pendant to no. 43.

Figure 102. *Poet. Roman marble head after a Greek original from the early third century B.C. Copenhagen, Ny Carlsberg Glyptotek.*

fig. 102 42 42

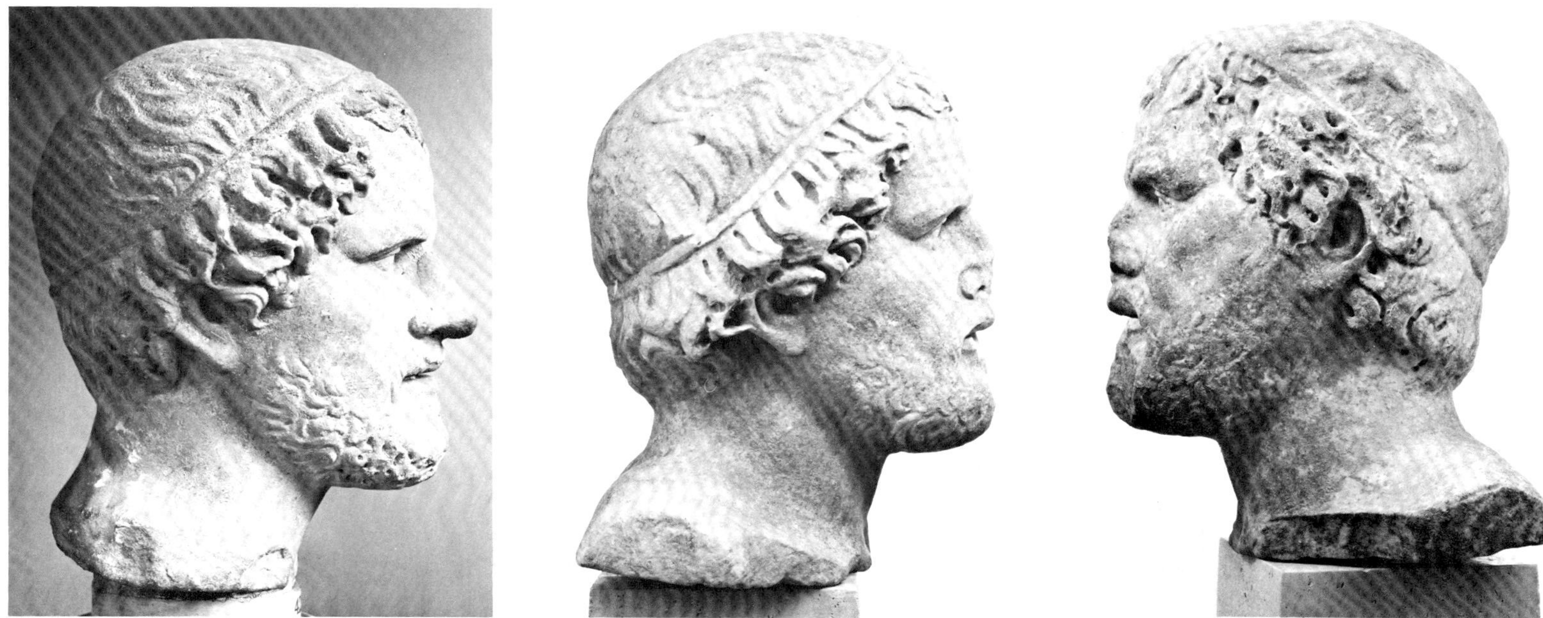

42. **Poet** A poet, characterized as such by the large taenia, must have been popular as he is preserved in an excellent copy in Copenhagen (fig. 102). The exterior marks of style and execution place the image in Athens, and more precisely close to the portrait of Demosthenes. The treatment of the beard in short locks is close to both Demosthenes and Phokion. The technique is identical with the next portrait with which it also shares recutting in antiquity.

43 43

***43.* Poet** This portrait is presented out of chronological sequence, because it belongs with the previous herm as a pendant, perhaps as part of a gallery. The technical workmanship is identical, with limited but clearly marked use of the drill in the curled locks of hair and beard and fair modeling corresponding probably to the Flavian period about A.D. 80. The sitter must have been a poet as, like his companion, he wears a fillet. His toothlessness, the sagging skin on his neck, and the dried up and ridged face muscles indicate advanced age. The ears have a peculiar and very distinctive shape. While his companion is rather joyful, he looks rather sour. A ruined replica, matching perfectly, is in the Capitoline Museum (fig. 103). It brings out a further point: the man, in spite of the different treatment of his physical age, is so much a kind of relative of the previous head (no. 42), that one wonders if the two portraits were not created as a gallery from the very beginning. The original can also be compared with the Pseudo-Seneca (fig. 86) and the philosopher (no. 6), thus dating from the first half of the second century B.C.

43

fig. 103

43. Poet

This old, toothless poet was carved as a pendant to no. 42; the workmanship of the copies is identical, enhancing the contrast between the originals. Both poets were restored in late antiquity.

Figure 103. *Poet. Roman marble head (surface recut, nose restored) after a second century B.C. original. Replica of no. 43. Rome, Capitoline Museum.*

44

44

44. Krates

A philosopher who intentionally neglected his appearance. A poor copy after an original of the later third century B.C.

45

45

45

44. Krates The late replica reduces both the plastic values and the individual characteristics of this portrait. However, this Cynic philosopher, a contemporary of Zeno, must have been a colorful personality. We know little about his doctrine, but there are numerous small anecdotes, evidence for the popularity of the man even in Roman times. Several copies exist; the better ones makes it clear that the sculptor was well aware of Silanion's Plato, but the trend toward genre, emphasizing the uncowed appearance of the self-neglecting philosopher is hardly possible before the rather late third century B.C., the nearest kin being the portrait of Antisthenes (no. 45), the founder of the same philosophical school. It was possibly created in the same circle of sculptors continuing the Attic tradition towards the Hellenistic Baroque. The original must thus have been a retrospective portrait. Our copy, rather poor in quality, brings evidence that the fame of the man lasted into the later Roman empire.

45. Double herm: Antisthenes and a poet There is very little of artistic value for either portrait in this small decorative piece other than the fact that this is the second time that the two faces are linked together in surviving antique portraits. Antisthenes, the true founder of the Cynic school, was once thought to have been portrayed close to his own time in the fourth century, perhaps even in the early part of the century. A recently discovered inscribed base provides the evidence that the original of his portrait type was created by Phyromachos, the exponent of Helenistic Baroque in Athens, at the very end of the third century B.C. Antisthenes is shown as an uncowed, rugged individual, but few of these qualities can be perceived in our replica.

His companion is a poet, as is clear from the large fillet in his hair. He, too, is well known in other replicas, one of them an over life-size statue, but his identity is not secure. He has been called Pindar because of the gravity of his general expression or, less probably, Archilochos because of his ebullience. The image is a pure *Fantasienbildnis*, belonging to the acme of Hellenistic Baroque in the early second century B.C. He appears together with Antisthenes on another occasion in the gallery in the British Museum found at Via Appia (poet: Richter, figs. 238–239; Antisthenes: figs 1058–1059) and with the three leading Epicureans: Epicurus, Metrodorus, and Hermarchos (Richter, figs. 1192–1194, 1237–1239, and 1303–1305). This is a strange combination, but our small herm confirms that it is not an accident. One would like to explain the association by the philosophical undertones of the grandiloquent poetry of Pindar.

45. Double herm: Antisthenes and a poet

Surprising combination of a fulminating poet (Pindar?) and a Cynic philosopher, perhaps because both treated mythology as moralizing paradigms. Unpretentious decorative work of the second century A.D.

fig. 104

fig. 105

Figure 104. ***Diogenes. Marble head (with restored nose and some recutting) replica of the second century B.C. portrait. The same man as no. 46 and fig. 105. Rome, Capitoline Museum.***

Figure 105. ***Diogenes with his beggar's bowl. Roman marble statuette reproducing the second century B.C. original. Afyon, Museum.***

***46.* Diogenes** This is an excellent replica of the late second century B.C., full of vigor. The artistic temperament of the copyist harmonized well with the Hellenistic Baroque of the original. Represented is the man who, when the impressed Alexander proposed to fulfill any wish he might have, immediately requested Alexander to move to one side to let the sun shine on Diogenes more fully. The identification is difficult as the only ancient evidence is provided by a miserable statuette known in two replicas; one divided between the Metropolitan Museum of Art and the Villa Albani, and the other unpublished in the local museum of Afyon (Turkey) (fig. 105), showing Diogenes as a beggar. Comparing our head and its replicas with these small statuettes is encouraging for the identification but not conclusive. The Renaissance and Baroque centuries liked this portrait very much; there are numerous reproductions of it, and one of them was even labeled "Diogenes." A beggar-philosopher, claiming absolute independence and living on the margins of his society, is in a way a romantic figure, but that is not how antiquity saw him. If there was some tradition of Diogenes' actual appearance—and the statuettes do not flatter the man—the face is dramatized but kept in the frame of what would normally be a genre image. The high Hellenism, like other Baroque periods, enjoyed the effect of combining pathos and the grotesque. A replica in the Capitoline Museum (fig. 104) has been badly mistreated.

46

46

46. Diogenes

Splendid Baroque image of the intentionally hirsute dog-philosopher. Unpretentious decorative work of the second century A.D.

47

48

47. Diogenes in his barrel

With his faithful dog on a Roman sarcophagus, Diogenes may be intended as a symbol of immortality reached by abnegation of worldly goods. Late second century A.D. after a Hellenistic prototype.

48. Herakleitos (?) as a learned Herakles

With a volumen of philosophical texts in his hand on a Roman sarcophagus: scholarship promises immortality. Mid-third century A.D.

***47.* Diogenes, from the short side of a muse sarcophagus** Muses in the later Roman tradition are often connected with philosophers. Any intellectual was promoted in this time to be homo spiritualis—*musikos aner*—a man inspired by the Muses (see also the next item). But Diogenes with his mocking humor, who was a man with his feet on the ground—the complete opposite of an aerial creature—seems to us a surprising companion of the Muses. But the Romans thought differently; here he is with his barrel home, beggar's bag, and faithful dog.

***48.* Herakles/Herakleitos? on the side of a Muse sarcophagus** That Herakles is intentionally depicted as a philosopher is evident from his appearance and from the volumen in his hand. This was a common idea from the Stoics on, but Herakles holds his rather unusually long, knotted club in a strange way and the face, with its long beard, looks rather like a portrait than like any of the customary types of the hero. The association of Muses with real philosophers is attested to by the decorated sides of other sarcophagi with the Muses. See for example the preceding representation of Diogenes (no. 47) or the seated Socrates connected with a Muse on a sarcophagus in the Louvre. The allusion to Herakles and to some extent the physical type may be proper for Herakleitos, whose doctrine seems to have come back into fashion by late antiquity—even fathers of the church aptly appropriated his teachings about fire consuming the universe on the last day.

49

50

49. Zeno

The Levantine founder of Stoic philosophy. The portrait combines personal anxiety and a taste for teaching. The original was from the third century B.C.

50. Kleanthes (?)

The second head of the Stoic school. Clearly a compatriot of Zeno, but more robust (a former slave) and better balanced. After an original of the third century B.C.

***49.* Zeno** Zeno, the founder of the Stoic school of philosophy, came from Kition in the Phoenician part of Cyprus. The portraitist responsible for his statue captured very well the ethnic characteristics of his non-Greek origin. The man appears worried, neglecting with some intent his appearance, uniting absolute introversion with an excellent ability to communicate his ideas and persuade his followers. As was common for statues of Greek philosophers, Zeno must have been shown seated; our replica preserves the corresponding inclination of the head. The original in Athens must have been erected immediately following Zeno's death in 263. Stoicism was the preferred philosophy of Romans; no wonder that so many replicas have been found; however, the complete statue has not been recovered. In its present state our replica is a ruin, but the execution was excellent, dating probably from the earlier part of the second century A.D.

***50.* Kleanthes (?)** The head was originally conceived as an independent bust. One replica of the same portrait is in the Prado, another in the Hermitage. The original was wrongly dated, sometimes even in the fifth century, but it manifestly represents a further development of Zeno's portrait. The features belong to the same ethnic type, the same general type of worried philosopher. The hair is slightly different, the face is less emaciated, and the character is made less worrisome. The identification with Kleanthes is thus the first obvious suggestion, as they shared ethnic origin and philosophical orientation. Also, Kleanthes was the second leader of the school and the portraits follow each other well chronologically. The usually proposed portrait of Kleanthes, known in several statuettes—of which only one has a head (Richter, fig. 1106)—seems rather to be Periander, as the statuary type corresponds to other images of the Seven Wise Men and the preserved head seems to be more an individual version of the Corinthian tyrant (Frel, *Contributions*, p. 39). On the other hand, the close affinity with Zeno causes some hesitation. Is it another version of the same man as in the case of Antisthenes? Furthermore, another portrait known in three replicas may also be recognized as being from Zeno's "family," and another bored man with a shorter beard may also have been a Stoic.

fig. 106

49

49

50

Figure 106. *Hippokrates (?) Roman marble face (back of the head, nose, and neck restored) after an Attic original from the end of the second century B.C. Madrid, Prado.*

***51.* Hippokrates** The identification of this portrait as Hippokrates is based on the fact that one replica was found in the grave of a Roman physician, and the pillar on which it may have stood had the famous Greek maxim occurring in Hippocratic texts: "Life is short while art is long." There are some difficulties with the identification, however. Hippokrates, the father of Greek medicine, lived in the first half of the fifth century. We cannot expect a tradition about his appearance to survive; thus an image which manifestly belongs to the end of the third century should be a reconstituted portrait, while our man looks very "real." The style is identical with the well-known Stoic Chrysippos, whose portrait was made in Athens by Timarchides at this time. However, a rather similar physiognomy appeared, sometimes very schematized, sometimes carefully rendered in engraved stones set in finger rings, often found in physician's graves. An excellent example in a private collection in Los Angeles, dating perhaps from the first century A.D., is reproduced here.

51

51

51. Hippokrates

The father of medicine in an imaginary portrait created by the same sculptor as the famous Stoic Chrysippos, perhaps even as an adaptation of this portrait from the end of the third century B.C.

52 52

52. Sophokles

Late Hellenistic readaptation of the fourth century B.C. portrait. The man gains in age but not in characterization. The original was one of the most popular Greek portraits in Roman times.

***52.* Sophokles** The head in its present state is a ruin, and its main merit is to represent the great dramatist in California. The original was considered by some archaeologists as if not contemporary then produced with immediate knowledge of Sophokles' likeness. but comparison with the other version (the so-called Lateran Sophokles), faultlessly dated in the 30s of the fourth century, shows clearly that the prototype of the Farnese Sophokles (so-called after the best replica) just changes slightly the appearance established in the fourth century, adding signs of age and perhaps some willfulness. There is, however, no further step toward real characterization, and the Farnese Sophokles comes from the comparison with the other surely not as the better portrait.

***53.* Terracotta statuette of Socrates** Dressed in a mantle which is stretched over his protruding belly, Socrates stands on a schematized Ionic capital. The characteristic face with pug nose may go back to the prototype preserved in the British Museum statuette (Richter, figs. 560–562), which still may go back to the first portrait of Socrates (early fourth century, Farnese type); the Lysippic type (Richter, p. 116) must have belonged to a seated statue.

53. Terra cotta statuette of Socrates

From the late first century B.C. Rather a toy than a portrait.

54

54. Demosthenes

Powerful and convincing image of the eighteenth century after a then newly identified portrait of the great orator.

54 54

***54.* Demosthenes** Comparison with the genuine Demosthenes (see no. 40) produces admiration for the modern version. It expresses much more strongly admiration for the great and unfortunate democratic statesman: he has so much fire and spirit. This is because the modern sculptor shared if not our ideas than at least their avatars, and expressed them in a late neoclassical way with some stroke of romanticism à la J.-J. Rousseau. The piece is not an intentional forgery but a re-creation, perhaps for a gallery of the great men of the past made in the eighteenth century.

55

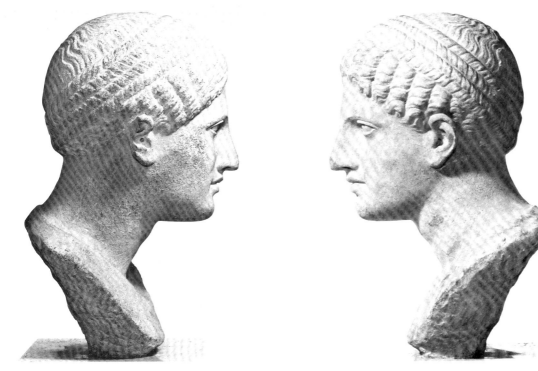

55 55 55

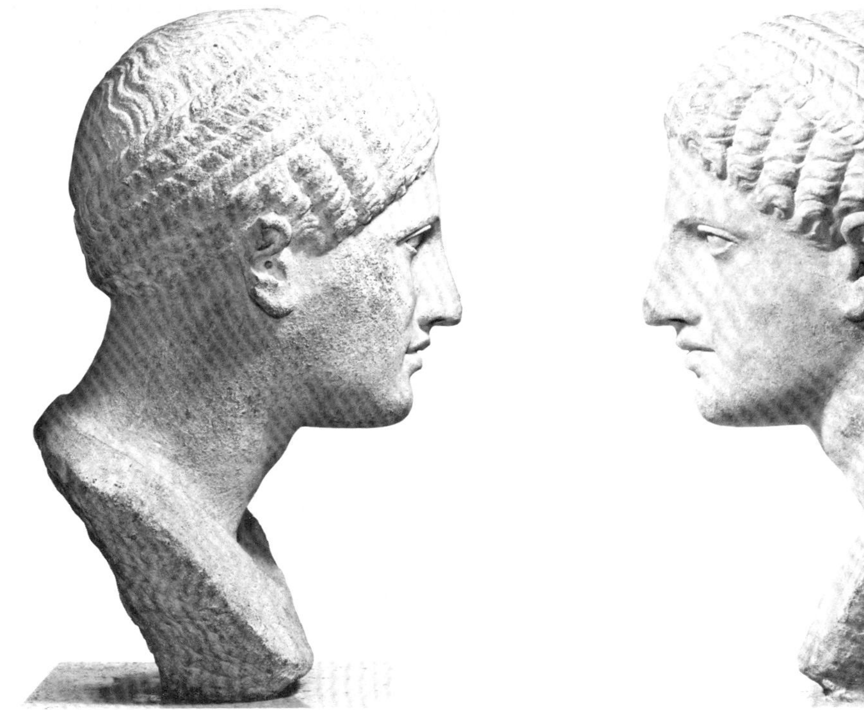

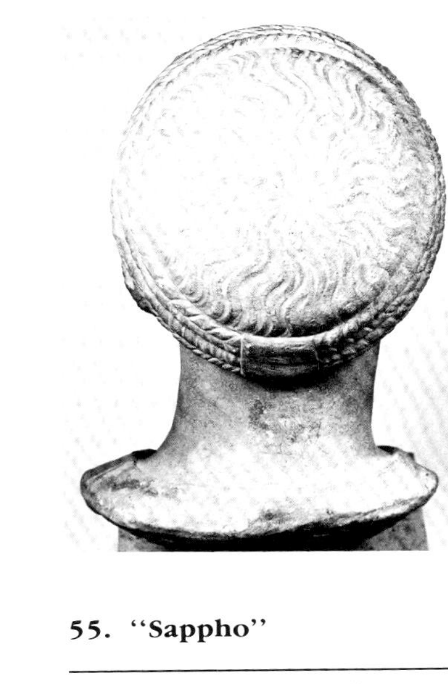

55. "Sappho"

Inscribed but unconvincing modern invention.

55. **"Sappho"** A portrait of Sappho by Silanion, the artist who created the statue of the seated Plato, is known to have existed; but no trace of it has survived. With this inscribed head, the lost Sappho by Silanion seemed to have reappeared. But even if the strange form of the name can be defended, the shape of the letters is rather odd.

Direct examination reveals several uncomfortable facts. The cutting technique is not ancient. The shape of the bust is without ancient parallel: its back is picked, and the edges are beveled slightly. The folds of the tunic and its neckline are unique. The modeling of the flesh is rigid and unorganic. The pattern of the hair from the cowlick on the occiput is not ancient. Both ears have strange, deeply drilled holes. The patina, including rootmarks, is artificial (concrete mixed with chalk). The large clip holding the four braids on the nape is without ancient parallel and has no clearly defined shape or function. It is evident that our Sappho is a very recent forgery.

56. **Statuette of a nude warrior wearing an Attic helmet** The bronze statuette was originally sold as a modern reproduction. Only after passing from the original owner's hands did it become "spurious," as the new owner assumed that it was ancient.

The original work of art is in the Barcelona Museum and represents a warrior, perhaps a general, with an Attic helmet. The statuette has been studied at length, but it seems not to have been noticed that the head reproduces a well-known type occurring in five replicas. The statuette gives us an idea of the body of the lost complete statue, probably correctly translated from a bronze original of the early fourth century.

All the other known Athenian strategoi wear Corinthian helmets. This one with an Attic helmet has been called Lysandros, the Spartan commander and politician who brought the Athenian empire to its knees in 405 B.C. But this proposed identification, based on the bull in relief on the helmet of one replica, is not entirely convincing, although the suggested dating to the end of the fifth century must be correct and is confirmed by the style of the body of the statuette.

56. Helmeted general

Modern cast sold by the museum that owns the original, after a genuine statuette.

SUPPLEMENTARY INFORMATION

1. Xanthippos
74.AA.41
Presented by Nicolas Koutoulakis.
Pentelic marble,
H: 40 cm.; h: 21.4 cm.

Crest and nose missing. Surface weathered, especially on the right side, to the point where the features are difficult to discern. Copious use of the drill. Antonine replica after a Pheidian bronze original of the middle of the fifth century B.C.
For the two replicas see: Berlin (figs. 38 above and 88), ex-collection Polignac: Pandermalis, p. 34f., pl. 8, 1–2; Ephesos (our fig. 84 above): Pandermalis, p. 35, p. 8, 4.
For the comparison with the portrait of Anakreon, see especially Richter pls. 5/6, figs. 285–5 and 288–90 and figs 36 and 38 above. Compare also an inscribed head of Kodros on a glass paste in Heidelberg which may derive from a Pheidian statue (R. Hampe, *Heidelberg, Neuerwerbungen*, 1957/60 (1971) no. 147, pl. 109 and A. Guiliano, *Xenia* 2, 1981, 59, fig. 5). *Checklist* 2, no. G7.

2. Statuette of a strategos
Private collection.
Bronze,
H(figure): 14.4 cm.;
H(head): 1.6 cm.

The plume of the helmet is partly broken off. Left leg twisted below the calf where there is a deep gash. The surface pockmarked overall. The eyes are inlaid with silver; the nipples with copper. Late first century B.C.
For the piece in the Wadsworth Atheneum, see E. Bielefeld, *AntPl* 1 (1962) pp. 39–41, pls. 50–57. *Unpublished.*

3. Strategos
75.AA.51.
Pentelic marble,
H: 30 cm.; h: 19.5 cm.

Point of helmet, left hair and eyebrow, and tip of the nose missing. Surface slightly weathered, especially on the left half of the face. The top of helmet and the back seem to have been carved separately and attached. Copious use of the drill, most noticeable for the parting of the lips.
The head is a circa mid-second century A.D. replica of the so-called Alkibiades (see Pandermalis, 59ff., no. 9, pls. 17–19). The original must have been from the same hand as the portrait of Philip II of Macedon (no. 4), thus by Leochares, circa 340 B.C. *Checklist* 2, no. G8; A. Herrmann, *AJA* 85 (1981) 234.

4. Philip II
75.AA.48.
White, probably Italian (Carrara?) marble,
H: 28 cm.; h: 22.6 cm.

Used as fill for masonry. Nose missing, several chips missing on forehead, left cheek, and beard. Deep drill marks in inner corners of eyes, ears, and parting of mouth (with teeth indicated). Once known as "Alkibiades," this type was proposed by Helbig for Philip II; the identification has been confirmed recently by V. von Graeve (*AM* 89 (1974) 231ff.).
Hadrianic to early Antonine replica after an original by Leochares, circa 340–330 B.C. *Checklist* 2, no. G9.

5. Philosopher
73.AA.44.
Said to be from Ostia, together with no. 6. Pentelic marble,
H: 38.5 cm.; H (head): 25.5 cm.

Point of nose battered, some chips; otherwise in a good state of preservation. Mantle over left shoulder slightly broken. Light drill work for nose, inner corners of eyes, and ears (none in hair).
The replica dates to the first century A.D. *Greek Art and Life*, exhibition Fogg Art Museum (March–April 1950) no. 187; Tozzi Gallery advertisement, *Burlington Magazine* 109 (1967) p. xxxix; Frel, *Contributions*, p. 34, pl. XII, no. 3; *Portraits*, pp. 13–14, no. 4, ill.; *Checklist* 2, no. G11.

6. Philosopher
73.AA.45.
Said to be from Ostia together with no. 5.
Pentelic marble,
H: 39 cm.; h (head) 26.8 cm.

The workmanship is slightly more cursory than no. 5, with copious use of the drill in hair, beard, and folds of the mantle and over the left shoulder. The back is rather summary. Both nos. 5 and 6 are not proper herms: the sides are roughly worked, which precludes the possibility of lateral prismata. No extant replicas exist of this head (contrary to what is stated in *Portraits*).
The replica is from the early first century A.D. J. Frel, *Bulletin of the Cleveland Museum of Art* (1970), p. 283, no. 7; *Portraits*, p. 14, no. 5; *Checklist* 2, no. G12.

7. Thucydides 1
76.AA.47.
Presented by G. and C. Fallani.
Fine-grain whitish marble,
H: 27 cm.; h: 23.2 cm.

Chin and nose broken off; both eyes, upper lids, right eyebrow, and mustache battered. The head was recut in antiquity: the beard, instead of being in curly locks, is now an undulating, compact mass, with the mustache also cut down. The hair on the right side of the head and left side of the nape was rearranged at the same time.
A Roman copy of an original from the third quarter of the fourth century B.C. *Checklist* 2, no. G13.

8. Thucydides 2
73.AA.36.
Presented by Nicolas Koutoulakis.
Greyish, grained marble (Thasos?)
H: 29.5 cm.; h: 26.4 cm.

Nose missing; the surface battered, especially on the left half of the face. The pupil is indicated by a hole. The replica must be from the advanced second century A.D. *Checklist* 2, no. G14.

9. Plato
81.AA.64.
White medium crystalled Asia Minor marble,
H: 13.5 cm.

Lower cheek, chin, and nose missing. Surface weathered. Traces of drill for corners of the mount and the inside of the ears. Despite this, it seems to be a Greek original from the first century B.C. *Checklist* 2, no. G1.

10. Plato
73.AA.16.
White marble,
H: 36 cm.; h: 18.8 cm.

Point of nose and part of helix of left ear broken. The surface is slightly weathered. Drill work in corners of mouth, beard, nose, inner corners of eyes, and the crescent-shaped holes of the pupils. Made for insertion in a seated statue. The replica dates from the early third century A.D. and is so spiritualized that it seems rather a variant than a copy after Silanion's original of the middle of the fourth century. *Portraits*, 12–13, no. 2, illus.; *Checklist* 2, no. G15.

11. Double herm; Plato and Aristotle
74.AA.15.
From Egypt. Large crystalled white marble from Asia Minor with blue layers running parallel to the join of both heads,
H: 38 cm.

The noses of both heads are slightly abraded, but the tips are preserved. Below Plato, the front of the herm seems to have been cut down at a late date with a claw chisel. On both, the pupils are indicated by a slight hole. The herm was intended to be used as a fence post in antiquity (see J. Frel and G. Schwartz, Getty *MJ* 5 (1977) pp. 170–173 esp.), thus neither artistic nor portrait excellence was important. The work dates to the early third century A.D. *Recent Acq.*, no. 14; *Checklist* 2, no. G16.

12. Aristotle
L79.AA.26.
Anonymous loan.
Pentelic marble,
H:32.5 cm.; h: 20.5 cm.

Battered, especially the left half of the face. Must have been imbedded in a modern wall. Good Flavian copy of the prototype usually attributed to Lysippos. *Checklist* 2, no. G17.

13. Aristotle
75.AA.105.
Anonymous donation.
From the Haurân. Haurân basalt,
H: 27 cm.; h: 21.2 cm.

Right occiput, nose, helixes of both ears, and right temple missing. Surface weathered; the spotted patina has been cleaned off. Deep cutting, perhaps by the drill, of the corners of the mouth, parting of the lips, and ears. Idealized so that the portrait elements are neglected. The copy dates to the later second century A.D. *Checklist* 2, no. G18.

14. Thespis (?)
75.AA.67.
From the Hauran. Hauran basalt,
H: 29.5 cm.

Surface slightly eroded. Later second century A.D. execution. *Checklist* 2, no. G19.

15. Euripides
79.AA.133.
Ex-Ernest Brummer (acquired by him in 1913).
Pentelic marble,
H: 34 cm.

Fairly well preserved with some chips and weathering. The copy may have been done at the very end of the first century A.D. *The Ernest Brummer Collection*, 16–19 October 1979, pp. 234–235, no. 630.

16. Herm of Solon (?)
73.AA.134.
Said to be from the island of Corfu. Ex-collection Professor B. Meissner, Zeuthen.
Pentelic marble,
H: 52.5 cm.

The hair on the back of the head has been washed with acid. The restored nose and some other restorations have been removed. The herm is without cavities for the lateral prismata. The replica may be Hadrianic.
Arndt-Bruckmann, *Grieschische und römische Porträts*, no. 1194/ 5; *Ars Antiqua* 3 (Luzern, 29 April 1961) no. 28, pl. 15; *Ars Antiqua, Lagerkatalog* 6 (June 1966) no. 1, pl. 1; Sotheby's, 5 July 1973, no. 95, pl. 31; *Recent Acq.*, no. 15; *Checklist* 2, no. G20.

17. Periander
74.AA.63.
Ex-collection T. Barlow-Walker Presented by Dr. and Mrs. Fred Bromberg.
Fine grained marble with mica, possibly Pentelic,
H: 24 cm.

The piece had been set in a modern herm with the inscription *MILO*. It suffered much modern retouching, which may explain the hesitation over its attribution. The plastic indication of the eyes is modern, as is the cutting up of the nostrils and tip of the nose and some areas of the hair and beard, including the patching of the surface with modern varnish and the holes drilled inside the ears to hold the stem of a modern bronze crown.
Parke-Bernet, 26–28 September 1972, no. 300; *Portraits* no. 45; *Roman Portraits in the J. Paul Getty Museum*, exhibition catalogue, Philbrook Art Center, 26 April–11 July 1981, no. 94 (there hesitantly called dubious).

18. Aischines
L79.AA.27.
Anonymous loan.
Pentelic marble,
H: 50.2 cm.

The front half of the herm is missing along with the nose. The front and left side of the head are badly battered. On the chest of the preserved half of the bust an inscription is deeply carved:

ΠΕΡΙ[ΑΝΔΡΟΣ
ΚΟΡ[ΙΝΘΙΟΣ
Μ]ΕΛΕ[ΤΗ ΠΑΝ

The inscription covered with the same patina as the sculpture is indisputably genuine, as confirmed especially by G. Daux (visiting scholar at the Getty Museum October–November 1980). The portrait is evidently a replica of Aischines whose identity is well-established (see Richter, pp. 212–215, figs. 1372–1390). The Hadrianic copy is of excellent workmanship. *Checklist* 2, no. G27.

19. Alexander the Great
73.AA.27.
Pentelic marble,
H: 28 cm.

The left ear is an ancient secondary intention carved into the hair. The strands of the hair and the lower eyelids were also redrawn at the same time, the right sideburn was shortened, and the surface of the face slightly repolished. This head and its companion Hephaistion (no. 20) below belong together with the head of a princess with melon hairstyle (fig. 97, 73.AA.29), the head of a flutist (fig. 98, 73.AA.30), and a head of a lion (73.AA.31); also twenty-five marble fragments of hands, feet, doves and apples (all 77.AA.2) plus an over life-size left hand (76.AA.35), a small left hand (76.AA.28), a finger tip (78.AA.301), and a right elbow (78.AA.309). They were all part of a probable funerary monument, possibly a cenotaph of someone connected with Alexander and his court. A similar case, slightly earlier, is the so-called Alexander sarcophagus from Sidon where Alexander and Hephaistion are shown hunting lions and taking part in a battle, in high relief on the sides of a coffin created for a petty local king. The Getty Alexander is clearly posthumous, and so is Hephaistion, as he did not live as long as his master and friend.
JPGM, p. 26, illus.; *Guidebook*, p. 20, illus.; *Checklist* 1, no. 20; C. C. Vermeule, *Greek Art from Socrates to Sulla*, pp. 55, 59, 126, fig. 71A; *The Search for Alexander*, exhibition catalogue, National Gallery of Art (1980), p. 101, no. 6, color pl. 2; C. C. Vermeule; *Greek and Roman Sculpture in America* (1982) no. 102.

20. Hephaistion
73.AA.28.
Pentelic marble of the same quality as Alexander,
H: 26 cm.

The marble of the disk forming the restored top of the head is of lesser quality. The hair was shortened, the pattern of the strands reworked, and slight repolishing of the lower eyelids when the head was restored in antiquity.
The identification of Hephaistion, proposed originally by B. Ashmole, is confirmed by the votive relief in Thessalonike Museum (see Vermeule, *Greek Art*, fig. 72) recognized by Ariel Herrmann.
Alexander and Hephaistion are associated on the Alexander sarcophagus from Sidon, in two insertion busts from Kyme (Istanbul: Mendel II, nos. 597 and 599) and perhaps in two heads made for insertion into statues: the Alexander from Kos (Istanbul: Mendel II, no. 539; *EAA* I 243, pl. 353) has a possible Hephaistion counterpart in Budapest [Frel] (Hekler, *Die Sammlung antiker Skulpturen—Museum der bildenden Künste* [1929] no. 36).

21. Statuette of Alexander
73.AA.17.
Said to be from western Asia Minor.
Pentelic marble,
H: 31.5 cm.

Head broken off. The left arm broken off; the right arm, which was carved separately and attached with an iron pin, has been lost. Legs missing. There is a small splinter of marble missing on the right back and at hairline. Tip of nose missing and face cleaned. The right arm was extended, probably holding a spear, while the left hung at the side. There is a pentimento on the left side of the chest where some of the surface was removed to fit the added arm in position. The statuette seems basically to be a mirror image of the type of Lysippos' Alexander with the Lance carved in the second century B.C. *Portraits*, no. 1, illus.; J. Frel, *The Getty Bronze*, p. 22, pl. 7; *Checklist* 1, no. 102.

22. Alexander
77.AA.3.
Anonymous donation.
From Alexandria.
Whitish homogenous marble,
H: 28 cm.; h: 19.2 cm.

Surface washed with acid and eyelids recut in recent times. The nose, mouth, and chin are broken off. Traces of drill in the hair. The hair with eleven holes for the insertion of metal rays. The head is common work of the second century A.D. *Checklist* 2, no. G10.

23. Small head of Alexander
78.AA.317.
Presented by Lenore Barozzi.
Marble with medium crystals (Paros?),
H: 9.9 cm.

Surface weathered. Agressively cleaned and nose and lips recut in modern times. The workmanship seems to point to the later Hellenistic period. On the top is a hole, perhaps for a meniskos. Second century B.C. *Checklist* 2, no. G6.

24. Statuette of a Hellenistic ruler, probably Alexander
71.AB.167.
Bronze,
H: 9.3 cm.

Surface badly worn. Right arm extended with the hand broken off; left arm lowered with a pelta (?, now lost) attached through a hole in the left palm. Drapery over the left arm and shoulder. Circa second century A.D. *Checklist* 2, no. G42.

24. bis. Alexander as Sarapis
81.AB.66.
Presented by Mr. B. Sarner,
From Alexanderia,
Bronze,
H:12.3 cm.

Solid cast. Some small damage. The patina and the metal correspond to other Alexandrian bronzes. *Unpublished.*

25. The Getty Bronze
77.AB.30.
From the Adriatic Sea.
Bronze,
H: 151.5 cm.

Lost wax bronze cast with some additions: copper nipples and possibly lips, olive crown may have been silvered. Feet missing. The lowered left hand probably held a palm branch as, for example, the marble athlete in Istanbul (Mendel I, no. 129, pp. 334ff.) or the Hellenistic grave relief found in the Kerameikos in 1873 (Collignon p. 147, fig. 80).

Time (12 December 1977), p. 22, illus.; H. Herzer, *Artemis Annual Report* (1977–1978) pp. 10–13, illus.; J. Frel, *The Getty Bronze* (1978); *Checklist* 1, no. 50; P. Moreno, in *Storia e civilta dei Greci VI, La crisi della polis*, ed. by R. Bianchi Bandinelli (1979) 695–702, pls. 68–72; C. C. Vermeule, *Greek Art from Socrates to Sulla* (1979) pp. 23–24, 96, 120, fig. 28; P. W. Lehmann, Getty *MJ* 8 (1980) 113–114, figs. 17–18; A. Guiliano, *Xenia* 2 (1981) 60; C. C. Vermeule, *Greek and Roman Sculpture in America* (1982) no. 59.

26. Herm of a Hellenistic ruler
L80.AA.82.
Anonymous loan.
Bluish marble with large crystals from Asia Minor,
H: 39.2 cm.

On both sides are cavities for the prismatic arms. Root mark traces on the surface. Old chips on the right breast, missing nose and part of both lips; old and new chips and scratches overall.

Head of the original statue turned toward the left. The hair is in rounded, schematized curls. The fillet is characteristic of Hellenistic rulers. The taenia on the original may have been twisted, as the two ends and the nape are much less wide than the section lying on the shoulders. *Unpublished.*

27. Demetrios Poliorketes
78.AA.267.
Presented by Gordon McLendon.
Pentelic marble,
H: 9.9 cm.

Tip of the nose broken off. Intended to be viewed slightly from the right. There are traces of red polychromy in the hair. There must have been a bronze taenia in the rather summarily indicated hair, thus identifying the subject as a Hellenistic ruler. Third century B.C.
For the portraits of Demetrios Poliorketes, see most recently P. W. Lehmann, Getty *MJ* 8 (1980) 107–116. *Checklist* 1, no. 51.

28. Ptolemy II
76.AA.72.
Said to be from western Asia Minor,
White marble with big crystals,
H: 40 cm.

Chin, nose, right forehead, and upper lip broken off; upper lip only partially preserved. Surface weathered, especially on the right side. Corners of the mouth, inner corners of the eyes, and ears show use of the drill. Adapted for secondary use: the hair cut down and picked, and two big cavities cut into the temples, and a "crown" of seven iron nails fixed in place above the forehead and five in the nape (some of them remain in the holes). Middle of the third century B.C.
For the identification, compare Kyrieleis, no. B8, pl. 13. On coins, Alexander the Great and also Demetrios I of Bactria are shown with elephant-head helmets. *Checklist* 2, no. G°.

29. Ptolemy III
78.AA.257.
Anonymous donation in the name of the Antikenmuseum, Basel.
White marble with large crystals,
H: 16.8 cm.

The bust is preserved to the middle of the chest, cut down from a statuette. Twelve holes around the hairline, two filled with stucco, suggest a gilded diadem that would have been attached separately. Late third century B.C.
Kyrieleis, pp. 168ff., 33ff., 145, no. C7, pl. 23; *Checklist* 2, no. G3.

30. Ptolemy IV (?)
78.AA.258.
Anonymous donation in the name of the Antikenmuseum, Basel.
Said to be from Egypt,
Grayish marble,
H: 13.5 cm.

Nose missing; numerous small chips and scratches. The hair on top of the head is very schematic. Around the head are traces of minor cutting to fit a crown in place. On the nape is a support pillar, standard for Egyptian practice. The features are midway between Ptolemy III (Kyrieleis) and Ptolemy IV. Late third century B.C.
Kyrieleis, p. 169, no. C10, pl. 25.1–3; *Checklist* 2, no. G4.

31. Ptolemy IV
78.AA.254.
Presented by Ira, Mark, and Larry Goldberg.
Said to be from Alexandria.
Marble with medium crystals (Paros?),
H: 11.5 cm.

Surface battered and abraded so that the face can scarcely be identified. Fillet originally around the head. The features seem to correspond to Ptolemy IV. Early second century B.C. *Checklist* 2, no. G5.

32. Head of a late Ptolemy pharoah
81.AA.164.
Anonymous donation.
Egyptian limestone,
H: 7.6 cm.; h: 3.0 cm.

Nose and center of the forehead missing. Weathered overall. On the back are incised measurements. First century B.C. *Unpublished.*

33. Head of a Hellenistic ruler
79.AA.56.
Bluish grained marble from Asia Minor with dark veins,
H: 34 cm.

A deep cut on the right side in the hair. Nose, chin, and much of the lips missing; numerous chips. The surface seems to have been cleaned with acid. Above the forehead are fine curls with drilled centers and separations; behind them is a thick fillet. There are deep drill holes in both ears (to anchor another, metallic crown?). The corners of the eyes, nostrils, and parting of the lips were drilled, and the pupil was once indicated with a small holes. These specifics, the overall technique, and the rather schematic workmanship help to support the identification as a second century A.D. copy after a third century B.C. original.
For the statuette in Kansas City (Nelson-Atkins Museum, Nelson Fund, no. 46–37; found at Benevento, H: 56.8 cm.), see C. C. Vermeule, *Greek and Roman Sculpture in America* (1982), no. 112. *Checklist* 2, no. G39.

34. Menander 1
72.AB.108.
Said to be from Asia Minor.
Bronze,
H:17 cm.

Inscribed on the cylindrical base, all the letters of the name can be traced: ΜΕΝΑΝΔΡΟϹ. The base is comparable to the bases of the small bronze philosopher busts from the Villa dei Papiri.
Ashmolean Museum, *Report of the Visitors* (1971–1972), p. 14, pl. 3; B. Ashmole, *AJA* (1973), p. 61, pls. 11, 12; *JPGM*, p. 41, illus.' *Guide*, p. 63, illus.; *Checklist* 2, no. G24; G. Hafner, *Prominente der Antike* (1981) 223ff. (denies the authenticity of the inscription without having seen it).

35. Menander 2
71.AA.120.
Said to be originally from Rome.
Fine grained white marble,
H: 51.5 cm.

The nose is a plaster cast after the replica in Boston; otherwise the face is intact. Traces of the original incrustation are well preserved. The back is roughly picked. A scratch on the right shoulder has been filled with plaster. Cavities for both lateral prismata are preserved: in the right one, traces of the original iron pin can be seen. Deep parting of the lips, upper contours of the eyelids, and hair and ears show copious use of the drill. A slightly schematic but powerful replica of the early Antonine period.
Catalogue, no. 16; Penn., no. 4, ill.; *JPGM*, p. 41, illus.; *Portraits*, no. 6; *Checklist* 2, no. G25.

36. Menander 3
73.AA.111.
Pentelic marble,
H: 57.5 cm.

The face is ruined by modern restoration. The mouth, chin, both cheeks, and even the wrinkles on the forehead are completely recarved. The broken off eyebrows are cut down. The eyes remain in deep shadow, their original shape preserved. This was once the best of the three replicas in the Getty Museum: the face is ruined, but the hair, although flattened, shows the original brilliance. An excellent copy of Hadrianic date. *Checklist* 2, no. G26.

37. Epicurus
73.AA.55.
Pentelic marble,
H: 37 cm.

Only the middle portion of the head survives, without the nose. On the nape, the mantle is preserved. The concave bottom surface of the neck seems to be ancient, thus from a bust although the shape is unusual for a Greek portrait. An excellent, ruined replica from the time of Trajan.
Portraits, no. 8; *Checklist* 2, no. G22; V. Kruse-Berdold, *Kopienkritische Untersuchungen in den Porträts des Epikur, Metrodor und Hermarch* (1978), Nachtrag, last page (but even if the work may look "östlich," it is indisputably Italian).

38. Epicurus
81.AA.73.
Presented by M. Wiener.
White, slightly grained marble,
H: 13.1 cm.

The nose is partially missing; otherwise the head is well preserved. The left half of the face is covered with a dark patina. Drill work is used for the corners of the mouth and in the ears. A good replica of the early second century A.D. *Checklist* 2, no. G23.

39. Philosopher
77.AA.103.
Presented by Heinz Herzer.
Pentelic marble,
H: 26 cm.

The surface is completely ruined. There is a replica in Florence (A. Melucco Vaccaro, *Prospettiva* 6 (July 1976), pp. 3ff., figs. 1–4, described as "Roman portrait of the third century," and *Boll. d'Arte* 37 (1972) fig. 12, next to p. 258, text on pp. 242 ff., dated Antonine). The original must have been inspired by the image of Aristotle (see Frel, *MMA J* 5 (1971), pp. 173–178, for another early Hellenistic portrait derived from Aristotle). The expression is milder, the style more classicistic than Aristotle, oriented rather towards the trend represented by the sons of Praxiteles and their portrait of Menander. Still, a good impression of introspection is achieved. Our copy must be Hadrianic. *Checklist* 2, no. G21.

40. Demosthenes
74.AH.30.
White, homogenous marble,
H: 34.5 cm.

The surface has suffered from rather extensive cleaning and the eyebrow contours seem to be partially recut, perhaps already in antiquity. Nose and chin missing; chips and scratches over the surface. The head was worked for insertion into a statue. The workmanship is rather cursory. Flavian replica. (The smaller head of Demosthenes, lent to the museum by J. Paul Getty, has been returned to Sutton Place [E. Diez, *MJ* 1 (1974) pp. 37–42; *Portraits*, no. 7].). *Recent Acq.*, no. 16; *Checklist* 2, no. G28.

41. Phokion
73.AA.112.
Grayish crystalline marble from Asia Minor (?),
H: 16.5 cm.

Surface slightly washed with acid but otherwise intact. Sharp traces of the drill in mouth and eye corners and left inner ear. The right ear is missing. The face is perfectly preserved, including the nose. The copy dates to the early second century A.D. *Checklist* 2, no. G29.

42. Poet
74.AA.8.
Companion piece of no. 43.
Pentelic marble,
H: 29.5 cm.

Nose missing and some chips on the surface. The nose, mouth, and ears are drilled. The copy is Flavian after an original of the time of Demosthenes, circa 280 B.C. On the right side in a secondarily picked area is an iron pin to hold a small prism in place. *Recent Acq.*, no. 17; *Checklist* 2, no. G30.

43. Poet
74.AA.9.
Companion piece of no. 42.
Pentelic marble,
H: 38.5 cm.

Hair chipped, and the tip of a very distinctive nose missing. The right top of the nape was worked as a separate piece and is missing. Both sides of the herm were cut down in antiquity and new lateral prismata attached with metal pins of which traces exist in the left side. A large shallow chip in the middle of the breast. *Recent Acq.*, no. 18; *Checklist* 2, no. G31.

44. Krates
71.AA.284.
Crystalline marble, perhaps Thasian,
H: 53 cm.

The portrait is a bust, an unusual shape for a portrait of a famous Greek. In the back a modern iron ring to hang the piece on the wall is still attached. Copious use of the drill overall, but the modeling is very flat. The replica must date to the early third century A.D.
Catalogue, no. 17.; *Portraits*, no. 11 (the restored nose now removed); *Checklist* 2, no. G32.

45. Double herm; Antisthenes and a poet
78.AA.378.
Presented by Idelle and Sidney Port.
Italian (?) marble,
H: 23.5 cm.

The reduced replicas have little artistic pretension and have been overcleaned in modern times. The double herm dates to the later second century A.D.
Parke-Bernet, 8 May 1976, no. 314; *Checklist* 2, no. G33; Stewart, *Attikà*, 28 n. 32.

46. Diogenes
73.AA.131.
Ex-collection Flammingo.
Marble,
H: 33 cm.

Several bad breaks on the nose, left eyebrow, and mustache. An ancient replica is in the Capitoline Museum, Stanza dei Filosofi (fig. 104, Arndt-Bruckmann, nos. 325–326; Stuart Jones, p. 228, no. 21, pl. 56), where there is also a third replica, recarved if not modern. For further modern replicas see Frel, *Bulletin of the Cleveland Museum of Art* (1970), p. 283, no. 7 and Madrid, Prado; main entrance (not to the gallery) of the Palazzo Doria; court of the Palazzo Torlonio in Via della Concilizazione, Rome; a plaster in the vestibule of the Palazzo del Te in Mantova; another one once in the possession of François Girardon (drawing reproduced in *GBA* 82 (1973), p. 48, fig. 59 where it is already named Diogenes); a bronze bust in the Louvre (*ibid.*, fig. 64), and another one on the London art market. The powerful replica in the Getty Museum is Antonine, while the original must date from about 200 B.C.
Richter, *Portraits* II, p. 185, fig. 1072; *Portraits*, no. 10; *Checklist* 2, no. G34.

47. *Diogenes on the short side of a Muse sarcophagus*
81.AA.48.
Anonymous donation.
White marble,
H: 41.5 cm.; W: 53.0 cm.

The Muses are missing their heads, and there are several breaks. The side with Diogenes is relatively well preserved. Late second century A.D. *Unpublished.*

48. *Herakles-Herakleitos? on right side of a sarcophagus with Muses*
72.AA.90.
Fine grained white Thasian marble,
H (approx): 137.5 cm.; W (of side):

On the incomplete front is a seated lady and four Muses: Terpsichore, Thalia, Euterpe, a sphere for Urania, and a Herakles mask and part of Melpomene. On the side in flat relief stands a Herakles as a philosopher. Circa A.D. 250–270.
Magna Graecia, exhibit May–June 1967, Galerie Kamer, New York, no. 29, illus.; *Catalogue* no. 90; *Checklist* 2, no. V40; C. C. Vermeule, *Greek and Roman Sculpture in America* (forthcoming 1982) no. 215.

49. *Zeno*
74.AA.34.
Ex-collections Miss M. C. Martin, England, and Professor Sanbery, Uppsala.
Pentelic marble,
H: 30.5 cm.

The modern bust and restored ears, nose, and lower lips have been removed. Some chips and bruises on the surface. Even in the ruined state, it was clearly an excellent Hadrianic copy. (The Capitoline head, Stuart Jones no. 86, is omitted in Richter's list of replicas.)
Sotheby's, 17 May 1965, no. 209; Sotheby's, 29 January 1968, no. 90; Richter, II, 188, no. 7; Richter, *Suppl.*, p. 20, figs. 1098 a–c; *Checklist* 2, no. G35.

50. *Kleanthes (?)*
78.AA.330.
Presented by M. Gottlieb.
Ex-collection Joseph Müller, Solothurn.
Pentelic marble,
H: 32 cm.

The left upper part of the skull, the back of the head, and the lower right part of the back of the head are missing. The surface has been washed with acid. The replica seems to be Hadrianic.
For the replica in the Prado see Blanco, no. 13–E, pl. 5; for the head in Leningrad see O. Waldhauer, *Ermitage*, no. 66. Christies, 14 June 1978, no. 138, pl. 28; *Checklist* 2, no. G36.

51. *Hippokrates*
73.AA.25.
Grayish, slightly grained marble,
H: 27 cm.

Abundant root marks on the right half of the head help confirm the authenticity. The ears are extremely schematic (as on the Budapest Thucydides). The surface is weathered. The workmanship is cursory, reminiscent of Demosthenes (no. 40 above). The drill was used for the upper edge of the nostrils and the parting of the lips. Some chips on the surface, but otherwise intact. This is a new replica of the early Trajanic period of a portrait preserved in five replicas (Richter, *Portraits* 1, figs. 855–868, add. an ancient face with a modern occiput in the Prado no. 259E; here fig. 106). *Portraits*, no. 9; *Checklist* 2, no. G37.

52. *Sophokles*
72.AA.157.
Pentelic marble,
H: 34.5 cm.

The surface was burned, leaving black traces on the left side and the surface partially cracked. Further spoiled by strenuous cleaning. The right side of the occiput missing a splinter. Countless chips overall.
Ars Antiqua (Luzern) (7 December 1962) no. 55, pl. 20; "The Arts of Antiquity," special exhibition, New Paltz, New York, no. 5, illus. on cover; *Portraits*, no. 12; *Checklist* 2, no. G38.

53. *Statuette of Socrates*
75.AD.27.
Presented by Noma Copley.
Said to be from Asia Minor.
Brownish homogenous clay with traces of white slip,
H: 23.1 cm.

There was originally a separate base under the capital, as there is a cavity. Compare the bronze Metrodoros in New York (Richter, "Epicurus," p. 199, fig. 1220). First century B.C./ first century A.D). *Unpublished.*

54. *Demosthenes*
78.AH.318.
Anonymous donation.
Ex-collection F. Trau, Vienna.
Marble,
H: 33.; b: 22 cm.

Surface slightly washed. Top and back of head missing. Abundant drill work in the hair. Head made for insertion in a standing statue. The agitated appearance of the forehead, the modeling, and the whole appearance are not ancient. The piece is nevertheless not a forgery but an eighteenth-century creation after the small inscribed bust found in 1757 in the Villa dei Papiri. *Checklist* 2, no. G43.

55. *"Sappho"*
79.AK.73 (ex 58.AK.10)
Anonymous donation.
Italian marble,
H: 38.5 cm.; b: 16.8 cm.

Inscription: **ΣΑΦ|ΦΩΙ**
The tip of the nose is slightly bruised and part of the ear helixes is cut off.
P. Wescher, *Bulletin, Getty Museum*, 1.2 (1959) 17ff., fig. 7; H. von Heintze, *Das Bildnis der Sappho* (1966) 10ff.; K. Schefold, *AJA* 71 (1967) 205ff.; A. W. Byvanck, *BABesch* 42 (1967) 142ff.; A. Garcia y Bellido, *ArchEsp* 40 (1967) 162; J. Frel, *Eirene* 7 (1968) 154–155 (the last four are reviews of Heintze's book); H. Jucker, *Gnomon* 41 (1969) 77ff. (states that W. Fuchs considered after direct examination that the piece is a forgery; considers the patina and root marks as genuine; with sophisticated methodology, he explains the irregularities of the inscription); H. Jucker, *AA* (1970) 490, no. 9 (the negation of authenticity is still to be proven but the head in Eleusis claimed as a replica by Heintze is not one); I. Linfert-Reich, *Musen—und Dichterinnen Figuren des 4. und fruhen 3. Jh.* (1971) 117, no. 4 (forgery); Richter, *Supplement* (1972) [5], figs. 252a,b; *Checklist* 2, 14, no. G44.

56. *Statuette of a strategos*
78.AB.411.
Anonymous donation.
Bronze,
H: 21.1 cm.

Missing: right hand and the supporting rivet under the left foot.
For the statuette in Barcelona see Pandermalis, pp. 84ff. (bibl.) and Garcia y Bellido, *AA* (1941) pp. 204–212. For Lysandros, see Pandermalis, 37ff., no. 5, pls. 9–10. For the new replica in the Musée Rodin, see *Rodin Collectionneur* (1967–68), no. 166. *Checklist* 2, no. G45.

ABBREVIATIONS

Catalogue: Cornelius C. Vermeule and Norman Neuerburg, *Catalogue of the Ancient Art in the J. Paul Getty Museum* (1973)

Checklist 2: *Antiquities in The J. Paul Getty Museum. A Checklist. Sculpture* II. *Greek Portraits and Varia* (November 1979)

(J.) Frel, *Contributions: Contributions à l'iconographie grecque* (1969)

Getty *MJ*: The J. Paul Getty Museum Journal

Guide: Guidebook; The J. Paul Getty Museum (1980, fifth edition)

Joys: J. P. Getty, *The Joys of Collecting* (1965)

JPGM: B. B. Fredericksen, et al., *The J. Paul Getty Museum* (1975)

(H.) Kyrieleis: *Bildnisse der Ptolemäer* (1975)

(D.) Pandermalis: *Untersuchungen zu den klassischen Strategenköpfen* (1969)

Penn: *Selected Works from the Ancient Art Collection of the J. Paul Getty Museum*, exhibition catalogue, State University, University Park, Pennsylvania (29 May–20 June 1971)

Portraits: Greek and Roman Portraits in the J. Paul Getty Museum, exhibition catalogue, California State University at Northridge (16 October–11 November 1973)

Recent Acq.: J. Frel, *Recent Acquisitions. Ancient Art. The J. Paul Getty Museum*, exhibition catalogue, Washington State University, Pullman, Washington (9–30 October 1974).

(G.M.A.) Richter, *Portraits: The Portraits of the Greeks* I–III (1967)

(G.M.A.) Richter, *Suppl.: The Portraits of the Greeks. Supplement* (1972)

(A.) Stewart, *Attikà:* (Supplementary Paper no. 14. Society for the Promotion of Hellenic Studies, 1979)

INDEX BY ACCESSION NUMBERS

77.AB.30	Getty Bronze	25
77.AA.103	Philosopher	39
78.AA.254	Ptolemy IV	31
78.AA.257	Ptolemy III	29
78.AA.258	Ptolemy IV (?)	30
78.AA.267	Demetrios Poliorketes	27
78.AA.317	Small head of Alexander	23
78.AA.318	Demosthenes	54
78.AA.330	Kleanthes (?)	50
78.AA.378	Double herm: Antisthenes and poet	45
78.AK.411	Statuette of strategos	56
79.AA.56	Hellenistic ruler	33
79.AK.73	"Sappho"	55
79.AA.133	Euripides	15
81.AA.48	Diogenes sarcophagus	47
81.AA.64	Plato	9
81.AB.66	Alexander as Sarapis	24 bis
81.AA.73	Epicurus	38
81.AA.164	A late Ptolemy as pharaoh	32

PRIVATE COLLECTION

	Statuette of a strategos	2

LOANS

L79.AA.26	Aristotle	12
L79.AA.27	Aischines	18
L80.AA.82	Herm of Hellenistic ruler	26